One of the Chosin Few

Best Wishes
Dave Brady

One of the Chosin Few

Dave Brady

A ROYAL MARINE COMMANDO'S
FIGHT FOR SURVIVAL BEHIND ENEMY
LINES IN KOREA

NEAT BOOKS

Published in Great Britain in 2004 by
James Neat Publishing, 91 London Road
Stanford Rivers, Essex CM5 9PN
Telephone: 01277-364611, E-mail: jan@neat522.fsnet.co.uk

© Dave Brady 2003

Technical support by Cathy Neat

Development Plus Consultancy
Martin Breese, Breese Books

Bill Hiscox, Korean War Museum
Brentwood, Essex, England

For permission to use the
41 Independent Commando Coat of Arms
a special thank you to Fred Hayhurst author of
Green Berets in Korea

All rights reserved

ISBN: 0-9547193-0-1

Typeset in 11½/14 Caslon by
Ann Buchan (Typesetters), Middlesex
Printed in Great Britain by
Athenaeum Press Limited

Contents

Foreword		vii
Preface		ix
Map of Korea		xii
Chapter 1	One Volunteer is Worth Two Pressed Men	1
Chapter 2	Orient Bound	7
Chapter 3	With the Losers of the Little Big Horn	12
Chapter 4	Final Preparations	21
Chapter 5	Down Under	27
Chapter 6	I Hear No Trains	35
Chapter 7	I'll Never Eat Rice Again	47
Chapter 8	New Shoes	58
Chapter 9	Goodbye McGill	62
Chapter 10	To Join the Marines	66
Chapter 11	Bitten Off More 'n We Can Chew	70
Chapter 12	Here Come The Chinamen	79
Chapter 13	Alone, All Alone	91
Chapter 14	Thank God For Percy	100
Chapter 15	Break Out	110
Chapter 16	Escape to Tokyo	122
Chapter 17	Sonjin to Hiroshima	137
Chapter 18	Wonsan Bay	150
Chapter 19	Gilhoully's Brew	160
Chapter 20	Goodbye Binnie	168
Chapter 21	The Little Chinese Gun	170
Chapter 22	Good Riddance	178
Roll of Honour		190
List of Illustrations		191

**To Catherine
for her support and encouragement**

Foreword

In 1950 Dave Brady was serving as an Assault Engineer (expert in demolitions, mines and defence works) in the Royal Marines when volunteers were called for to form a commando unit for service in Korea. Initially employed on raiding the North Korean coast, after the breakout following the Inchon landings, 41 Independent Commando joined the United States Marine Division in the drive for the Yalu River through the inhospitable 7,000 ft. mountains where the screaming North wind from the Russian Steppes reduced the temperatures to a numbing minus 56 degrees.

Dave Brady tells how he was isolated after an ambush when the Chinese hit the 1st. Mar. Div; of his encounter in the snow with a Chinese soldier and of how he made his way through enemy territory to the relative safety of a U.S. Marine Corp outpost. This is one Britisher's story of the great fighting withdrawal of the fine Marine Corp's Division from the mountains to the sea.

Subsequently the book recounts how 41 Commando operated from bases inside the Communist held harbour of Wonsan some sixty miles behind the main battle line. Throughout, the story is spiced with tales of friendly rivalry between the British and American soldiers and of brushes with authority of both nations.

Brady quickly establishes himself as the unit 'wag', always ready with an apt remark, usually at an inappropriate moment. This account of his service with a remarkable force which maintained high morale despite heavy casualties is told in an amusing, self deprecatory style with none of the false heroics often associated with books of this kind.

After leaving the Royal Marines, Brady joined the Metropolitan Police and was presented by the Sovereign with the Queen's Gallantry Medal for his part, while unarmed, in the arrest of armed robbers. His book 'Yankee One and George' recounts some of his experiences in 25 years of police work was published in 1984. (Plans for second edition by Neat Books)

Colonel Peter Thomas
41 Independent Commando
The Royal Marines

Preface

Prior to the second World War, Korea was an integral part of Japan. It was intended that after the defeat of Japan, Korea would be established as an independent state. Russia entered the war towards the end of the conflict. As Communist forces moved south from Russia, American forces travelled north up the peninsular. The opposing armies met on the 38th parallel which passed across the land at about halfway. Here a line was established as a temporary border, which, as the years passed, hardened into a permanent line between the two politically different halves of the state. The north became the People's Democratic Republic and the south the Republic of Korea. The Russians retained a strong presence in the north and the Americans maintained token occupation forces south of the parallel.

There was considerable antagonism between north and south as their political stances hardened. The north had a huge Russian-equipped army under the command of its president, an army officer, General Kim il Sung. The army of the south was pitifully armed in comparison.

On 25th June 1950, after a number of 'Border Incidents', the North Korean army launched a massive invasion led by a strong force of T34 tanks of Russian manufacture. They quickly brushed aside weak opposition. The United States sent to Korea its occupation army from Japan. This army had grown soft through years of easy duty in occupation and were no match for the hard-bitten Communist troops, and were eventually pushed into a small enclave in the south-east of the country around the city of Pusan.

The Russians, were, at this time, boycotting the United Nations and in their absence a resolution was passed which allowed the members of the United Nations to come to the assistance of the South Koreans. The Russians could not veto the resolution because of their absence from the Security Council.

Korea is, in the far north, mountainous and inhospitable, with no major roads through the mountains. The main line of communication and supply between Vladivostock, in Russia and the communist front line was a single-line railway track which hugged the east coast. This very important supply line consisted of many long tunnels through the coastal mountains and was not vulnerable to air strike or bombardment from the sea. It was obvious that it would require attrition by forces landed from the sea to curb the war supply situation of the communist forces. Further, to guard the coast against raids by aggressive commandos would require many thousands of North Korean troops who could more usefully, from the enemy point of view, be employed elsewhere.

The Royal Navy was committed to the war, and they were the only organisation amongst the United Nations forces troops capable and trained to fulfil attacks from the sea on the all-important east coast railway line. These forces were the Royal Marine Commando units. There was a brigade of these elite marines already in action, in Malaya against communist forces there. The Malayan War was being won by the British Army supported by the Commando Brigade.

When the request was received for the raiding unit to go to Korea it was decided not to weaken 3 Brigade and therefore a small highly trained group of 200 commandos were formed from various Royal Marine Commando units in the United Kingdom and elsewhere.

They grouped at Plymouth and were eventually flown to

Japan where for reasons of supply, they were equipped with American gear. The United States troop-carrying submarine *Perch* and two assault personnel destroyers, *Wantuck* and *Bass* were placed at the disposal of the new unit. Thus was born, the 41st Independent Commando Royal Marines.

The unit was smaller than a normal Commando and contained a higher than usual quota of specialists due to the tasks they were to be asked to perform. The vast majority of the unit were operational troops; the disadvantage of this policy became apparent when in November 1950 the unit suffered 50 per cent casualties and no reinforcements were available for some time. By chance, these casualties decimated the specialist sections of the unit which curtailed raiding activities for many months. The specialists consisted of:

- *Assault engineers*: They were highly trained in demolition techniques under commando raid conditions. Generally it was to get these specialists ashore that the whole organisation of the raiding unit was tuned.
- *Heavy weapons*: The term 'heavy weapons' was a misnomer because the heaviest weapons used had to be capable of being carried on the back of a marine: 81mm mortars and light and heavy machine guns were the prime weapons used to support the unit during the raid. Whilst in a static role on the Wonsan Islands they used 75mm recoilless rifles to harass the mainland Chinese.
- *Signallers:* Both short range and long-range signal capabilities were required for contact between individual sections and with supporting ships at sea. As most operations were at night and visual signals could not be used, the efficiency of communications was essential for success.
- *Swimmer-canoeists*: Highly specialised and trained commandos used for reconnaissance. Lonely work requiring considerable initiative and personal courage.

The Korean name for their land is CHOSEN translated as; 'The land of the morning calm.'

THE BATTLE OF THE CHOSIN RESERVOIR
(CHOSIN FEW)

On the road between Hagaruri and Kotori, in North Korea, near the Manchurian border, Royal Marines of 41 Independent Commando and men of the U.S Marine Corp fought a fierce battle in temperatures below minus forty degrees, with a Chinese Army of 120,000 soldiers who had crossed the border and poured over the mountains, both sides sustaining horrendous casualties. The surviving Marines are known as 'The Chosin Few.'

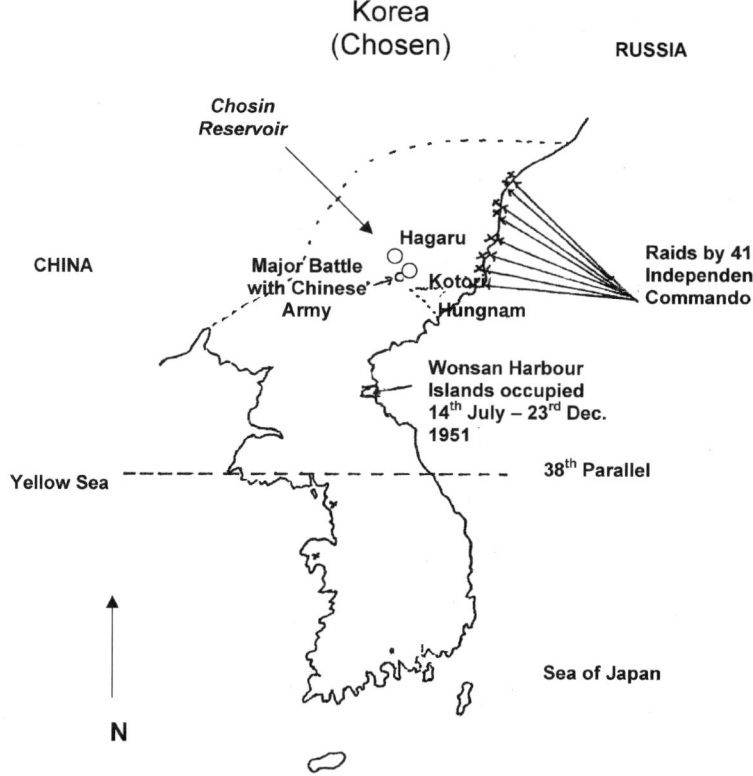

CHAPTER ONE

One Volunteer is Worth Two Pressed Men

Among the students eagerly assembled, of diverse nationality and rank, his eyes shining, his swarthy features agog with enthusiasm, stood the Egyptian army lieutenant. His dark complexion was one point that differentiated him from the others, who were junior officers of various armies, though mostly from NATO countries. The other feature that drew my attention to him was the fact that his uniform gaiters were on upside-down, giving his legs and feet the humorously incongruous appearance of a person wearing shoes on the wrong feet. It was an early day in August 1950, tropically warm, the heat of the sun bouncing off the grassy swards above the crumbling cliffs of Sandown, on the Isle of Wight, and reflecting on the calm shimmering seas of the English Channel.

No holiday scene this, for the waters contained a fleet of various small military craft, gathered around the base of the cliffs, their purpose to transport aggressive Royal Marine Commandos to the rocky coastline. This was a demonstration for visiting officer cadres, from around the world, of commando techniques for assault landings on inhospitable shores. The whoosh of rockets as they thrust grapnels into the air, dragging writhing climbing ropes behind them. The grapnels arched towards the cliff tops searching for a secure hold. The thump of mortars providing fire for the ant-like Commandos as they inched their way to the cliff top, eager to do the most awful mischief to those above!

Twelve thousand miles to the east, a victorious North Korean army was blasting southwards on the peninsular of Korea, pushing the battered South Korean and American forces into a small enclave around the main port of Pusan. They had invaded, without warning, some weeks earlier. It was the first armed assault by a communist country upon a non-communist neighbour, since the end of the Second World War and the reds were winning!

The officers gathered around a Commando Sergeant on the Sandown cliff top. 'Gentlemen, here you can see our method of rapidly transporting either prisoners, casualties or equipment, from the cliff top directly into a landing craft when there is no available beach to assist evacuation.'

He pointed to a wire cable anchored firmly to the cliff top, stretching over a pair of shear legs and out across a 150-foot abyss until it disappeared into the sea some 200 yards offshore. 'A landing craft will, at the appropriate time, move under the cable as we lower a small metal cage, suspended on a pulley, down into it.'

I stood at the cliff edge, singularly bored by the entire proceedings. My task was to guide the winch operator who lowered the cage, as he was back from the edge and could not see the surface of the water below. As a commando assault engineer my life was, under normal conditions, a cacophony of bangs, as, with explosives, I was allowed the happy task of disintegrating everything in sight at the slightest provocation. This particular task was the one assault engineering operation I found onerous.

Meanwhile, the war in Korea was being lost, the United Nations command was screaming for assistance and a number of

ONE VOLUNTEER IS WORTH TWO PRESSED MEN

countries of the 'Free world' were formulating plans to assist, hopefully before it was too late.

'Right!' The commando sergeant was attempting to display an enthusiasm he obviously did not feel. 'I want one volunteer to take a trip in the cage and be lowered into a landing craft.' The assembled group looked somewhat askance at the rickety cage, which was, in reality an open topped wire mesh box, within which only a complete nutcase would allow himself to be dangled 150 feet in the air!

'Here Sir.' The ungainly Egyptian, eyes gleaming with enthusiasm, took a stamping military step forward. He was eager to indicate to the surrounding soldiers, that Egyptians, contrary to popular belief, were not without considerable courage. He stood smartly to attention, his chin thrust in a Mussolini-type pose, his upside-down gaiters positively quivering with anticipation!

As I gazed at the Egyptian easing his rather plump body into the close confines of the cage, I could sense the opportunity of a release from the boredom I felt. I smiled inwardly, perhaps the day was not going to be so bad after all! With a gentle rumble of the winch, the swaying cage commenced its somewhat ungainly descent. Beneath the large peak of his uniform cap it was possible to discern that the worthy oriental gentleman had paled visibly, his brown knuckles whitening as he firmly gripped the sides of the swinging projectile.

It was, at this stage, that I should have waved the waiting landing craft into position beneath the cable, but, for a reason that escapes me, I did not immediately do so, I lingered a while. The cage swayed, the pulley whirred and the cable sang, as did I. Rapid assessment assured me that there was insufficient time for the landing craft to reach its allotted position prior to the arrival of the cage. It was fairly obvious that the Egyptian had come to the same conclusion for he began to panic. Egyptian panic, unlike its British counterpart, which is conducted with the maximum of phlegm, is a fairly physical exercise. This physical agitation caused the cage to gyrate alarmingly. My boredom had completely disappeared. In fact I was feeling quite elated.

The coxswain of the landing craft increased the speed of his flat-bottomed craft, aware that should there be repercussions to the impending disaster, I would be able, with a little white lie or two, to apportion the majority of the blame to him!

There was a loud, terrified shout from the Egyptian. The only phrase I know in that language is *'Shuftie kush'* which has, I believe, a sexual connotation. The Egyptian definitely did not shout *'Shuftie kush'*. Whatever he had intended to shout, further ceased in a shower of bubbles as, with a gentle splash, the cage continued the journey beyond the surface of the sea. For a brief moment the cage and the Egyptian disappeared completely. I frantically waved the winchman to reverse. My joy turned to horror when an Egyptian army hat bobbed to the surface and floated away. I felt that there was a distinct possibility that I had drowned the poor inoffensive bastard! As the winch reversed, the cage reappeared with, to my inordinate relief, the Egyptian gasping and blowing like a large fish in a net. I could hear the running footsteps, behind me, as the sergeant closed on my rear. We stood side by side as the victim was dragged aboard the landing craft by its crew. They were somewhat amused!

'You prat!' a voice roared in my ears as the red-faced sergeant forced his larynx so that he could be heard above the guffawing of the assembled soldiery. I stood, stiffly to attention, as he tore me up, publicly, for arse paper!

'It was a simple miscalculation by the landing craft, Sarge.' I mumbled the first stage in my defence, trying it out as it were.

'Miscalculation my arse . . . you will see the troop commander in the morning.'

He stomped off, followed by the chortling young officers. His shoulders were heaving, whether with laughter or anger it was difficult to tell. The stitches holding my corporal's stripes in position began to fall apart before my very eyes! Wouldn't it be strange had the officer's name been Gemal Nassar? I could have inadvertently built antipathy to all things British in his mind, which, some five years later, would lose us the Suez Canal . . . No? Perhaps not, but what a lovely thought!

In the Pusan area of Korea a perimeter was established and the North Koreans were being held at bay, with some difficulty. Signals flew from the War Office and the Admiralty as preparations were put in hand to organise a British contribution to the war.

At six o'clock on the evening of the Egyptian debacle I relaxed, horizontal on my bunk. It didn't look too good, my only hope was to blame the coxswain of the landing craft, but be had lots of witnesses. All looked black.

'Corporal Brady.'

'Yes Sarge?' He didn't look too up tight, perhaps it would be okay after all.

'The troop commander will see you . . . now, at once!'

Now that was really bad news if it couldn't wait until the morning. I nipped from the hut and strolled, very, very slowly, across to the Troop Office. To my surprise there were about ten other assorted commandos loitering outside, later I realised they were all specialists in some Commando activity or other. At that stage I presumed they were to be witnesses to my demise!

I marched smartly into his office, saluted and waited.

'Aaaah, Corporal Brady.' The relish in his tones boded ill for me.

'Sir!' My mind became a blank, I would have to play it by ear.

'There is a small independent commando unit being formed at Plymouth. They are all volunteers. Pack your kit now and join the draft which will leave here this evening. Okay?'

Not a bloody word about the Egyptian Officer.

'Right, sir.' I turned as smartly as relief would allow me, and marched towards the door.

'Oh, just a moment, corporal.'

'Shit!' I thought.

'The unit will be going to Korea very, very shortly. That is all.'

I fled. The words did not really penetrate. I sat on my bunk.

'Korea?' I thought, 'Korea? There's a bloody hairy war going on out there . . . that's a bit heavy for ducking an Egyptian!'

As I packed my kit and prepared to leave for Plymouth, it suddenly occurred to me that the troop commander had said that it was an all-volunteer unit. I had been eight years in the Marines, seven of them spent with commando units. I knew better than to volunteer for anything. I rose and, as casually as possible, wandered across to the sergeant's quarters.

'Sarge?'

'Yes, what do you want?'

'About this Korea business. It's a voluntary mob and I didn't volunteer.'

'You have now,' he grinned, 'unless you want to discuss the small matter of the attempted drowning of an innocent Egyptian . . . do you?'

'I've just volunteered,' I replied disconsolately.

'Good boy,' he smirked. 'Now piss off and let me get some kip.'

CHAPTER TWO

Orient Bound

The following morning, on my arrival at the Royal Marine Barracks at Plymouth, I joined a group of a hundred or so assorted commandos who had appeared from all over the country and from various commando units. One thing we had in common was that we were all specialists in our particular fields: assault engineers, heavy weapons experts, signallers and swimmer canoeists. All were quite experienced and mature men. I met lots of old faces from the past. I was pleased now that I had 'volunteered' the affair had, at first sight, the possibilities of a fair amount of excitement, I certainly wouldn't have to take liberties with innocent Egyptians to relieve the monotony from hereon in!

We were to be interviewed as to suitability for the new unit. I joined the queue. Having seen the calibre of the waiting marines my attitude had changed, I wanted to go, I would consider it a personal insult were I rejected! Finally I was ushered into a large room with the minimum of formality, which in the Royal Marines was unusual. There, seated at a trestle table, were three officers. The senior, new to me, was Colonel Drysdale, the CO of the unit. Seated next to him was Captain Pat Ovens, a byword in commando assault engineering techniques. I had served with him in the past in various commando units. His nickname, to the troops, was Percy. My heart sank a little when I saw him, as I was aware that he didn't care greatly for my attitude. It was a serious business which I had, on occasions, been guilty of treating with an improper lack of decorum! I did not blame him, if I were an officer in a disciplined organisation such as commandos were, I would not have cared for me either!! The third officer was a Major Aldridge, a granite faced man, who looked tough as a commando was supposed to look, with a sardonic sense of humour. Behind him, epitomising everything that was good about the commando forces, was the RSM, 'Sticky' Baines. He wasn't overly enamoured to see me either, though beneath his stern exterior I noted the faintest semblance of a smile as I pleaded my case. I know Sticky Baines and Pat Ovens so well and was aware that they were extremely efficient and a cut above some of the idiots we could have been lumbered with. The interview was short, a general probe of my experience and capabilities. I was reasonably confident, I did know my job well. By the time I had saluted, turned about and marched out I had well and truly volunteered and been accepted!

I joined the hundred or so who had been accepted, milling about outside the hut. I was delighted. Lots of old mates, characters all and some of them very hard men indeed! I was pleased to be on their side. Most of them, I discovered, had volunteered in exactly the same way I had, with some bastard pointing a finger at them and roaring, 'You'll do!'

When a small independent commando unit is formed it is usually to supply an Army with a small highly trained force, for clandestine operations, usually at night. For this reason they are lightly equipped when compared with a normal line unit. Though highly disciplined, emphasis was placed on the ability, when required, to act on personal initiative. They are by no means huge square-jawed men, but one thing could always be guaranteed, if you took them on, you were to be graced with a large mittful of trouble from a group of very well trained and fit bastards!

Off to the stores, where, surprise, instead of being issued tropical equipment, we were issued with ill-fitting civilian clothes, which I am sure originated from prison service discharge stores ... we looked like recently discharged convicts.

The unit we were forming was to be known as 41st Independent Commando Royal Marines and the only information imparted was that we were, after a very short leave, to be flown to Korea. Air travel in 1950, particularly a 12,000-mile journey, was an adventure indeed. Most troop movements were by ship, but we were needed quite urgently. The package holiday and cheap air fares were, then, events of the distant future and commercial jet airliners a figment of the imagination. I was quite pleased about the entire business. The fact that it might culminate with an angry North Korean attempting to stick a bayonet into my lovely body had not permeated through my brain, at this stage. The immediate future, as I saw it, was to revel in the fleshiest of the orient. Beyond that my mind refused to ponder!

A short leave at my parent's home in Liverpool and, at long last, dressed in my discharged convicts' gear, as were we all, except, of course the sartorially elegant officers, we bundled noisily into the terminus at London Airport, which was fairly primitive in those days.

At the airport we were met by a bowler-hatted paragon of the British upper classes. He smelled slightly of expensive aftershave, considered in those days by the Marines to have a slightly 'poofish' aroma.

'Gather around chaps.' His cultured tones trembled a little as a loud fart emanated from the group. He cleared his throat and shuffled just a little nervously.

'Right chaps. You may be wondering why you have been issued with civilian clothes and are travelling in civilian aircraft. I am here to tell you. I am from the Foreign Office and am here to advise you as to certain aspects of the journey you are to undertake.' He looked round anxiously. He had nothing to fear, he had captured our attention. 'You will be enter certain countries who do not allow British troops to overfly their airspace, let alone land for refuelling at their airports. Equally we do not want it to be made known that a unit such as yours, is bound for Korea, for obvious reasons. Therefore, you will, if asked, say that you are a travelling football team, on tour. You are aware, I am sure, that air travel is very expensive and used only by those who can afford it. I therefore ask that you do not draw attention to yourselves.'

As we boarded the four-engined Argonaut, which would take three days to reach the Far East, with two overnight stays, we were aware of a large number of pressmen photographing our embarkation . . . so much for foreign office security!

An enjoyable journey produced only one incident of import, when, at Karachi, whilst dining in some luxury at an airline hotel, accompanied by a string quartet, the waiter, dressed in all the British Raj gear, including a large turban, leaned over my shoulder and whispered conspiratorially, 'You are football team, yes?'

'Yes, that's right.'

The waiter placed a brown finger alongside his nose, adopted a quizzical expression, and said, 'Plenty fucking football teams come through here lately!' and nodding his head he wandered off to continue his chores whilst we stared at him in blank amazement.

At last, weary, we arrived in Hong Kong where we continued our journey by a rickety RAF Dakota aircraft, a far cry from the luxury of BOAC Our prison civilians had been taken from us at Hong Kong, we were back in uniform, as were the officers, and the status quo been re-established. In the year of 1950 the airport for Hong Kong was at Kai-Tac, the runway was very, very short and surrounded by mountains. I didn't enjoy the take-off one little bit, particularly after a large moustachioed RAF 'Hooray Henry' guffawed, 'Don't worry about a thing old boy. We nearly always get off without a prang!'

We discovered that we were not flying direct to Korea, but at first to Japan, we were to be stationed near Tokyo to enable us to reorientate to American weapons and equipment. Good news. Tokyo would suit me beautifully, for a while!

CHAPTER THREE

With the Losers of the Little Big Horn

As the craft bumped down on the runway at Tokyo airport it was dark and the lighting at reception illuminated a gathering of American army personnel waiting for us. There was no time to peruse the locals or to imbibe the oriental mysteries we were expecting, we were bundled into US army trucks and trundled away. Anyone who has travelled in the back of a military truck knows that vision outside is restricted to those fortunates who are able to grab a seat near the tailboard. I was not lucky. As we bounced about on the hard suspension of the trucks I wondered what lay ahead. I had experienced warfare in Europe but was a little uneasy about the situation I had become involved in here. We were silent, I looked at the glum faces of my new mates, most were relatively experience marines and knew what to expect. We would be happy when we could get cracking and do that for which we were paid!

As we entered what we were to discover was a barracks near Yokosuka, just outside Tokyo, and disembarked, we saw a huge sign which expounded to the world that this was the home of the 'US Seventh Cavalry' I don't know whether I was too happy at this stage to be involved with a regiment whose main battle honour in the past was a tremendous cock-up at the Battle of Little Big Horn!

The trucks squealed to a halt alongside a large wooden construction which was to be our home for a little while. As we offloaded from the vehicles, a gaggle of Yank soldiers lingered and watched. Though the Seventh Cavalry was currently serving in Korea, there were a couple of Companies of the regiment on leave and training at the barracks. A large sign told the world that we were in 'Camp McGill' by courtesy of the losers of the Little Big Horn. It came as a relief to me that I eventually discovered that the modern Seventh Cavalry did actually have tanks and infantry and had, many years before, discarded their horses.

As we settled in we decided to establish the portion of the barracks in which we had staked our claim, as a British precinct, complete with a large Union flag fluttering from a flagpole. Patriotism is nowadays a dirty word, but we were tremendously proud of what and who we were. We also established the criterion that Yanks were welcome, but only when invited. Another anathema which we did not tolerate lightly, was to be addressed as 'Limeys', the general consensus being that it was normally intended as a derogatory description in the same ilk as when we referred to Frenchmen as 'Froggies', so 'Limey' was definitely a no-no, as the cavalrymen were soon to learn.

The quarters were good and the American PX store, their equivalent to our NAAFI displayed goods of tremendous quality, very little of which we could afford.

Already our green berets were in short supply when we realised that in the quest for souvenirs, Yanks would pay the proverbial earth. Our boss 'Duggie' Drysdale soon resolved this problem. We had, on our arrival been completely re-equipped by the Yanks. The only British item we retained was our green berets. The governor ordered that, in the future, any member of the unit 'losing' his beret would not have it replaced and would instead have to wear the inner liner of an American army helmet. This remedy was psychologically sound, because the culprit would look to all intents and purposes like a US soldier and would be the subject of much piss taking by the other Marines. It worked, the loss of berets was reduced dramatically.

By now we, in the hastily assembled commando had become more acquainted with one another and friendships had developed, friendships, usually with blokes from one's own section. My section was 'S' Troop of the commando, which contained mostly the specialist troops of the unit. I was with the assault engineer section. Our function was, mainly, to destroy, with explosives, the targets the unit was to attack. Our brother section was the mortar and machine gun outfit. As a raiding unit we were very lightly armed in comparison to a line unit. We had the ability to operate for short periods with only what we could carry. We had little motorised transport and no weapon larger than that which could be toted on a man's back.

My 'run ashore' mates were Bill Taylor, who was, many years later to become my brother-in-law and whose cousin I was to marry, and Jerry Maill. They were both sergeants in the Mortar section. Bill was a man of quiet humour and reliability, Jerry, also taciturn, was a Geordie who was seldom found without a smelly pipe, exuding rank tobacco smoke, which made close proximity to him a 'cough-making' exercise. Both men were stocky and fit. Bill loved to approach his off-duty moments placidly; I was slightly more exuberant.

At long last, after a few days settling in, we were free for our first night out in Tokyo. We shaved, showered and counted our cash. The rate of exchange at that time was 1000 yen to the pound, so one didn't have to have higher mathematics to work out our financial state. We poured from the barracks, some in liberty trucks, but Bill, Jerry and I travelled on a Japanese bus, eager to catch the flavour of the Orient as soon as possible.

How polite the Japs were, and they displayed tremendous curiosity at the discovery that we were British. It came as a constant surprise to me that the Japanese, at that time, always concluded the discovery with the remark that all English were considered to be gentlemen. Eventually the bus dropped us in one of the main streets in Tokyo, the Ginza. Japan was, in those days, not the ultra-modern industrial society that it is today. The Yank influence was just starting to wedge into their way of life, but had not, as yet, destroyed their oriental quaintness.

We stumbled thirstily into the first bar we came across. We had tasted the American beers in their PX canteens, but were eager to taste the quality of the Japanese product. No pint mugs here, just as well really, because as we swallowed our first glass of Asahi beer we laboured under the illusion, soon to be disproved, that it didn't seem either as palatable, or as potent, as its British counterpart. As we staggered from bar to bar we were overwhelmed by the generosity of the other customers, mostly American servicemen. We always insisted on paying our corner but it could easily be described as a scrounger's paradise if one was so inclined.

We finally settled in a bar, at a table by a large street window overlooking a busy Tokyo street. I noticed as I gazed at the passing scene that the Japs were ultra-polite to one another, with continuous bowing, interposed with a jabber of conversations when they first met. I noted that *'Dom arrigato'* was the Japanese for 'thank you', and the response sounded something like *'Do tashey mashtay'*. Throughout my time in Japan, I used the response 'Don't smash the ashtrays' and it worked, and it was understood by the Japanese.

The milling crowds of Japanese and US servicemen produced a portrait which was quite unique. The old and middle-aged Japs were dressed traditionally in sombre clothing, all of the same cut. They were responding politely to the somewhat brash Americans but were extremely subservient. Were these the fearless, cruel nation that had fought the last war so unscrupulously? The attitude of the younger female natives, some in gaudy kimono and others in cheap western regalia, was friendly in the mercenary way of most women in occupied territory since the history of war began. They brought back memories for me, of English women, during the Second World War, sniffing around the Italian POW's in Lancashire whilst their kin were being killed by Italians in North Africa. Strange creatures!

Jerry, Bill and I were, by now, just a little in our cups! The bar was smokey and crowded. Jerry heaved himself to his feet, mumbled incoherently through his teeth which were clamped onto his beloved pipe. He disappeared in a cloud of smoke.

'That's not bloody fair,' I slurred to Bill, my speech not too articulate as my vocal chords struggled against the rising tide of the Asahi beer.

'What's not fair dear boy?'

'That's not fair.' I pointed out into the street, where I saw a slight, short Yank sailor being manhandled by four very large American sailors. He was fighting manfully, but there was no doubt that he was to be the eventual loser. He was so small and they so large, that sympathy for the apparent underdog evoked, within my drunken brain, a desire that justice should be done. I rose from my seat, settled my beret firmly on my head and prepared for battle.

'Keep an eye on my beer, Bill mate.'

'Leave it alone Dave. Sit down and mind your own business,' replied Bill, struggling to stand up, but subsiding gently as the swilling beer within him overcame his equilibrium.

'No . . . that's definitely not fair.'

I stumbled across the bar, bounced off one or two tables and staggered out into the street. The fracas was unabated and with a roar, I charged in to assist the poor little matelot. Through the flailing fists, I suddenly noted, with dismay, that the four large sailors had 'Shore Patrol' bands on their arms. The large yellow letters 'SP' caused instant consternation, because nobody with even a modicum of sense, tangle with US Military Police, because they are mean bastards with very little sense of humour, as was to prove the case.

The wee sailor, the reason for my drunken intervention, taking advantage of the unexpected assistance disappeared into the night, careless as to my fate and no doubt delighted to have escaped retribution for the offence which had caused him to fall foul of the Shore Patrol in the first place. He didn't even say 'Goodbye'. With very little preamble, and no doubt annoyed at the escape of their prisoner, the MPs quietly and methodically beat me into a subdued, bruised pulp.

As I flew through the air into the back of the MPs truck, my last sight was of the delighted Bill, a huge smile on his face toasting my abject stupidity with a large swig of my beer! He raised his empty glass in salutation and then fell back into his chair, laughing like a drain!

As we trundled through the night I thought of dear old 'Sticky' Baines the RSM, who would, at the news of my downfall, twinkle with ecstasy, fingers clawed to tear the stripes from my arms. What a prat I had been. As I wallowed in self-pity, slumped and dwarfed by the large MP's in the mumble of conversation in which they were involved I was fairly sure I heard the word 'Limey'. This roused my patriotic fever to such an extent that I roared out the first line of the chorus of 'Rule Britannia'. 'I'll give them Limey,' I thought. A gentle tap with a nightstick on my right cheek caused a rapid cessation of aggression as I once again subsided into semi-consciousness.

I was dragged, by now completely co-operative, from their vehicle and with an MP on each side of me, joined the rear queue of miscreants and escorts before a high desk at which sat a huge black sergeant, his beady eye and aggressive hunch exuding malevolence to a frightening degree. He glared at me as my turn arrived.

'Name!' he barked.

'Bloggins,' I replied.

'Unit?' I did not immediately reply.

'Unit . . . bastard!' He slammed a huge fist on the top of the stout desk which quivered slightly, as did I.

'Four One Commando, Camp McGill,' I quaked.

'You a Limey?'

I saw red, but now was probably not the time.

'No, I'm not. I'm British mate.' My snarl was slightly muted.

The aggressive sergeant leafed through a manual on his desk, gave me a long intimidatory stare and reached for the telephone. As he lifted the 'phone to his ear I noted that his fingers were like very large black puddings. If he was proportionally built, I thought, then one or two Japanese women must have had a heart rendering shock since his arrival in their country!

'This is the US Army stockade in Tokyo, we got one of your guys here.' He spoke very quietly; it was apparent that, whilst dealing with the law abiding, he was quite a gentle fellow.

'Name of Bloggins,' he continued.

He paused for a while, listening intently, then he covered the mouthpiece of the phone with an enormous hand. 'Is your name Brady?'

'Yes.'

He returned his attention to the phone. 'We'll hold him here until you send an escort.' The Sergeant then replaced the phone and spoke to my M.P. escort, 'The Limey tells lies, put him down!'

I pondered a brief moment on the possible meaning of the Americanism 'put him down'. I was not aware that it merely meant that I should be placed temporarily in a cell. In my bemused state, I presumed that it was a Yankee euphemism, indicating that I should be given a fairly decent smacking for my temerity in telling untruths. Realising that all was apparently lost, I decided that meek acquiescence to a thumping was not on, not at any price!

'Rule Britannia ...' I started. But, by now, my escorts were aware that this patriotic enunciation was a prelude of impending aggression on my part ... thump! That bloody nightstick had come into play once more. I was somewhat surprised that they seemed, when wielding their clubs, to always aim for the head of their target. Very effective, but quite dangerous I thought. I was somewhat dazed. My face and head were quite sore. I recognised the feeling of partial numbness and a gentle tingling sensation in the region of my right eye, which, coupled with a certain dimness of vision, indicated that I was the proud possessor of a magnificent black eye!

I rested for a while in the cell; it seemed but a moment,

'Hullo Dave, you silly sod.' The familiar accent heartened me. I had had quite enough of the nasal Yankee twang. I opened my good eye. There, before me, smiling broadly, were Sid Moon and Jack Foulkes, a sergeant and corporal from my section.

'That is some eye you've got there.'

We walked out of the cell, along a dimly lit passage and past the large black sergeant.

'See you, guys,' he waved in a friendly fashion, transformed by the presence of my mates from a man-eating ogre to a gentle giant. I did not acknowledge or agree with his salutation, I had absolutely no desire to see him ever again.

As we drove into Camp McGill, past the large Seventh US Cavalry sign I was heartened and relieved to see, in the distance, the fluttering Union flag. Beyond the flag I could see white sheets hanging from the first-floor windows and see the waving arms of my mates above the sheets. As we drew closer I could hear cheering and laughter and deciphered, in large black letters, the words painted on the sheets: 'WELCOME HOME KILLER'.

I fell about with laughter, grimacing as the muscle movements in my face accentuated the pain from my damaged eye. 'Rule Britannia ...' I started to sing, then involuntarily ducked as I remembered the beloved nightsticks of the US MPs.

The delights of my first run ashore in Japan now over, it was now retribution time. I was arraigned before 'Duggie' Drysdale, to the absolute delight of RSM 'Sticky' Baines and the expressed disgust of Percy Ovens. I received a tremendous bollocking and my record was noted 'Severely reprimanded', my stripes surviving yet again.

CHAPTER FOUR

Final Preparations

At last we settled down to the purpose of our visit to the oriental delights of Japan. The fighting troops were issued with US Garand rifles, self loading and heavy, with slightly smaller calibre ammunition than our old British rifles had used. The other specialists and I were presented with 'carbines', which could be best described as mini-rifles; not at all clumsy as were the heavy Garands. They were, however, as we were subsequently to discover, quite useless and not guaranteed to cause the enemy to always fall over when hit. For that rather important reason they were rapidly abandoned later on, when under war-like pressure. At the first opportunity they were replaced, the heavy Garands being purloined from others who had become *hors de combat*.

Now that we were re-equipped the training began in earnest. Being experienced marines, it took very little time to master the strange weapons and even less time for we assault engineers to familiarise ourselves with the American explosives and demolition equipment, which was, at that time, infinitely superior to its British counterpart. Particularly useful were the 20-pound packs of plastic explosive with detonating cord leads protruding which enabled the packs to be joined together rapidly. Ideal for our type of work, which was always done in a hurry!

One indication, to me, of the sanctity of human life in the US services, where equipment was the primary sacrifice and loss of life way down the list, were their booby trap switches. These items were designed to actuate an explosive charge, either by pressure upon them, the release of pressure or a pulling motion as from, for instance, a trip wire. The British devices had only one safety pin. We were well used to these. If the trap was incorrectly set up, in rare and extreme cases, the removal of the pin could actuate the explosive, this, from the operator's point of view, would be fairly unsatisfactory, particularly as it would probably kill him! None of this for the Yanks! Each of their devices had two pins, and if upon removal of the first pin the second could not be removed, then this indicated a possible malfunction in a much less drastic way than the British device . . . we liked it!

One morning, after parade, we were introduced to yet another piece of equipment. In the past we had become very adept at embarkation techniques from a myriad of types of flat bottomed landing craft, which were always engine powered. It came as a wee bit of a surprise to see, lined up in our compound, rubber boats . . . squat, lozenge-shaped, ungainly looking and quite large. I looked in vain for the struts to which outboard motors could be attached.

'What's the propulsion unit on these bastards, Sarge?' I pointed to the unseaworthy-looking monsters.

'There's your fucking propulsion unit.' The instructor smiled as he reached into the boat, and with a triumphant leer waved a wooden paddle over his head.

'Engines make noises and noises we don't want, so for the next few weeks you are going to paddle and paddle, for mile after mile, always in the dark, not along rivers, but out there!' He pointed towards the sea.

Paddle we did, 12 men to a boat, five each side, sitting on the rubber gunwale, with a bowman, and a coxswain at the stern. We paddled for hour after hour. Our technique rapidly improved, we became fitter. The fitter we became the heavier the load carried became and the faster we progressed. Christ, it was hard work, pitch black, just the view of the back of an equally tired marine, the paddles probing in and out of the sea. The gentle splash of the paddles coupled with the grunts of exhaustion from the crew the only sound. I was amazed by the fluorescence of the sea when the paddles disturbed the surface. No scenery to take one's mind off the trauma of mile after mile of travel. It was backbreaking, soul-destroying labour. The strangest piece of equipment aboard was a large, empty biscuit tin, which was nailed to the top of a broom handle. We were much too knackered even to ask what it was for. We would, in future, find out!

We practised silent landings on the coast of Japan. Crawling ashore, dragging our boats up onto the beach, unloading our gear. Playing at laying explosive charges on the Japanese railway lines and then quietly stealing away. It is fairly obvious that to lay a couple of pounds of explosives on a railway line is fairly ineffective and easy to repair. Our intentions were more lethal and entailed the lugging of literally hundreds of pounds of explosives to and from the boats. At least when it was real we wouldn't have to reload the bloody stuff!

As our paddling arms grew stronger and stronger our leg muscles suffered from their confinement, in the bent position, whilst paddling for hours on end. We cursed the boats, we cursed the paddles, we cursed the swelling seas and rocky beaches, but most of all we cursed our officers, who, at the end of a gruelling row, when we were completely exhausted and virtually collapsing on our arrival at the practice area, quietly informed us that we had another five miles to paddle. We were becoming fitter and angrier all of the time.

We had always trained to attack, and our equipment was designed to destroy, European-type railway lines. The startling discovery was made that we relied on our booby-trap switches to actuate the explosive as the target trains passed over the charges, at the same time they should not be visible to casual inspection of the line by the enemy, but the Japanese railway lines did not have the 'give' of European rails. In fact there was insufficient downward movement of the rail to actuate the pressure switch with the passage of a train over it. Percy resolved this by appending a perpendicular spike to the top of the pressure switch that passed between the gaps in the rails to protrude a minimal distance above the horizontal line of the rail. A cunning system of metal fulcrums, designed by him, ensured that the pressure of a man standing on it would not actuate it . . . after all we did not wish to waste 300 pounds of plastic explosive on one fellow! The 300 pounds were necessary to lift the train clear of the track.

Meanwhile it was still paddle, paddle, and more paddle. We could now travel for miles in fairly rough seas with the lead boat performing the navigation. It must have appeared strange to see five fat rubber boats each containing twelve marines, tied together bow to stern, slogging across the Japan Sea, looking somewhat like the humps of the Loch Ness Monster! To alleviate the fact that our legs were not much in use whilst paddling, our governors re-introduced us to the activity peculiar to commando and airborne troops, a torture called 'speed marching'. My introduction to speed marching had occurred many years earlier at the Commando School at Achnacarry in Scotland. It was as painful then as it was now! Fully equipped, 100 yards fast trot, followed by 100 yards rapid march, then 100 yards fast trot and so on, *ad nauseum*. Extreme exhaustion made the travelling of more than fifteen miles at a time, whilst speed marching, absolutely impossible. It was little wonder that at the culmination of training, all of it in the dark, we were totally unenthusiastic about extra-mural activities. Our sole recreation was to stagger across to the Seventh Cavalry beer hall, there to quaff copious quantities of Yankee beer and to engage in what was known as 'Sods' operas. This was where the Yanks began to realise that our music had nothing of innocence or sentimentality and the words were primarily concerned with various functions of the human body, either singly or together! Whilst in one corner the juke box was warbling 'Goodnight Irene', for the benefit of the Yanks, we were, in the other corner roaring in unison, such gems as 'She's a big fat bastard, twice the size of me'.

The song referred to a young lady known as Salome, who, in the song, always stood there with her arse all bare! The accompaniment was usually provided by 'Binnie' Barnes on his banjo. Poor Binnie was subsequently to die, I have never since been able to listen to a solo banjo without regret at his passing, because he was always a happy man whom I held in high esteem. The session usually ended with a rousing chorus of 'Roll a Silver Dollar, down upon the ground'. We were so aggressively fit that rarely did we tangle with the Yanks. There were, however, odd moments of light relief, when a large American soldier, armed with a sharp machete, stormed our part of the barracks, screaming like a dervish for the blood of the Limey marine who had, in the not too distant past, given the American's wife one! Or perhaps even two! He was disarmed and deposited outside British territory, still clutching the pair of trousers he had found on the floor of his wife's bedroom near an open window. All that he had seen of the offending marine was his bare arse protruding from his flapping shirt tail as he made good his escape. It was felt that an identity parade would be quite unsuccessful, as, I am reliably informed, one arse looks much like another.

At last, one evening a bustle of activity indicated that perhaps the shit was shortly to hit the fan. We were advised that we should pack all but that which was required under combat conditions. The rubber boats had disappeared from the compound, taken away by American sailors. We checked weapons, ammunition and other items, none of which indicated other than warlike propensities, and dumped our unwanted kit in a storeroom.

'This is it.' The rumour buzzed through the unit. We were full of mixed emotions, mostly of joy though, because surely whatever we had coming to us could not possibly be worse than the training we had endured.

We marched to a convoy of US Navy trucks, happy and noisy. As they moved off we let out a roar of delight. We were saying goodbye to Camp McGill and the US Seventh. There may well have been a few tearful eyes in the married quarters of the Seventh, but none from us!

CHAPTER FIVE

Down Under

As the US Navy trucks squealed to a halt we were aware that we had passed into a US naval base, probably Yokosuka. The tailboards clanged noisily down and, as we jumped onto the quayside, the first out stopped, mouths agape, to be shunted from the rear as more bodies spilled out of the trucks. Noisy conversation spilled from the ranks, with one voice, louder than the others hoarsely enunciated, 'It's a Yankee submarine!'

It was indeed. A brightly coloured 'Stars and Stripes' flapped noisily against the jack stay in the light warm summer breeze. The raucous howl of the sea birds, busily quarrelling over a titbit, vied with the bustle on the upper deck of the sub, where Yank sailors were milling about in their preparation. I gazed with a mixture of wonderment and apprehension, unable to relate our presence on the quay with the threatening-looking vessel. 'U.S.S. PERCH' . . . the letters bright and clear against the grey painted hull. It was a fairly large ocean-going submarine, with one unique difference from any I had seen before. Abaft the large conning tower was a huge cylindrical compartment, a hanger, the doors of which were wide open and into which the sailors were loading rubber boats, paddles and all the paraphernalia we had been training with for so many weeks. I could also see a powerboat in the hanger. Suddenly all of the hard work, paddling mile after mile in the Japan Sea, in the dark and under constant exhortation, 'In-out, in-out, faster, faster', from the governors, the pushing of our stamina beyond what we considered the norm, all came clear at last. I must admit that at the time I was not over-enthusiastic, I had been a marine for eight years. I was as happy as a sandboy on or above the sea. I was less than keen to operate under it!

'Sod this for a game of soldiers.'

'Why can't we have a British sub?'

However, beneath all the concern was a swirl of interest. Ah well, at least it might be something different.

High on the bridge atop the conning tower were two or three figures. Yankee naval officers. One waved, shielding his eyes from the sun with his had, he called out, 'Welcome aboard fellahs, welcome aboard.'

As we trooped across a narrow gang plank and down a hatch into the well-lit bowels of the boat, the ship's broadcasting system started to whine and then the music started. A female voice warbled in our ears:

'It's the little things you do that count,

They are only little things but how they mount,

Whilst I'm chopping down a tree, you always wipe my brow for me,

It's the little things you do that count!'

The hillbilly music was pleasant and cheerful and we discovered later that this was one of the theme songs of the ship's company of the *Perch*.

We had a number of theme songs in 41 Commando. One of which was suitable for mixed company. It was called, 'Roll a Silver Dollar' and was in honour of our special allowance of a dollar a day whilst attached to the US raiding forces. We had another type of theme song:

'She's a big fat bastard, twice the size of me,

Hairs upon her belly like branches of a tree.

She can run, jump, fight, fuck,
Wheel a barrow push a truck . . . etc. etc.'

Now wasn't the time to sing. The Yanks would hear it soon enough so we relaxed, chatted and listened to their music. 'Hi, this way youse guys.'

This from a rather tubby, friendly-looking matelot. He was of pale complexion as are most submariners; he was also very sincere in his attitude. He waddled ahead, unencumbered as were we, with weapons and kit. With some difficulty we headed forward towards the brows. The hum of machinery was accentuated by the smell of heavy oil permeating through the boat. Suddenly we all slowed, the most delicious smell of food wafted over us. We were like the Bisto kids in the advertisement. I would have followed that smell to kingdom come. We were passing the galley. There, sizzling tantalisingly, were the biggest steaks I had ever seen.

'For you, for you!" called a large sweating cook in immaculate white gear. He pointed to the steaks and then towards us. His appearance and accent made me think of chuck wagons on the prairie. I could, in my mind's eye, see him banging a triangle, screaming, 'Come and get it!' to the cowboys. I felt the pangs of greed clutching at my stomach, and I hurried forward, through compartment after compartment. At last our plump guide hove too and we stopped. There crammed into what had once been the forward torpedo room were rows of bunks. There were ten tiers, six bunks high all the way up to the bulkhead. The black hole of Calcutta must have been spacious in comparison. The bottom bunks were about three inches from the deck and the top ones very, very close to what landlubbers would call the ceiling. The crush was unbelievable, with milling marines jostling for position, kit being thrown in all directions. Throughout, the hillbilly music was still blaring,

'It's the little things you do that count.' The marines were getting a little cross to say the least.

'Move your arse, Bill, for Christ's sake.'

'Take your rifle butt out of my ear you prat.'

'This is fucking impossible,' shouted Rex Swancott, a swimmer-canoeist frogman. He stretched his mighty arms and with no difficulty cleared a space for himself. His bulk, and the displacement of ten marines by his movement increased the crush to panic proportions.

'Settle in your bunks, guys, until we sort ourselves out,' shouted our Yankee guide.

Whilst others rushed for the lower bunks I grabbed one at the very top. I considered carefully that from the top there was only one way that gravity would allow seasick to fall, that was downwards. I had no desire to share the bottom bunk with gallons of involuntary spew, cascading from above. It was much later that I discovered that there is nothing as gentle on the stomach than a submerged submarine-smooth and soporific!

In the close confines of an upper bunk I struggled out of my combat jacket, banging my head on the deckhead and cursing. Fortunately we were not wearing heavy cumbersome boots, but instead, whilst engaged on rubber boat training, had been issued footwear known as coral shoes. They were tough but of lightweight canvas and rubber. Not at all suited to conventional warfare, but ideal for quiet, fast, night movement, which was what we required. I bundled my carbine in my recently removed jacket and tucked in at the head of my bunk. Its disadvantage was it's short range. I hopefully did not intend any Korean to get close enough to use it, not with my long legs capable of twinkling along at a fairly rapid pace.

'Come on down, and bring your weapons with you.'

I cursed the Yank speaker and struggled yet again to unwrap my gun, more bangs on my head from the bulkhead and then the long climb down the bunks to the deck. Off we went again like lambs following our guide, back the way we had just come. As we passed a compartment on the port side a Yank relieved us of our weapons and stacked them in a small storeroom.

The Tannoy system clicked on . . . 'Now hear this-now hear this. Chow down, chow down. Royal Marines to the galley . . . chow down.' I remembered those huge steaks and we stampeded towards the galley space, following our noses. I do believe we may have trampled our guide to pulp in the stampede.

There, waiting for us was old 'Chuck Wagon'. A large, segmented tin tray was thrust into my hands. The saliva flowed as mouth-watering grub cascaded onto the tray from the waving ladles of the cooks. Slap! a huge steak hit the tin. I gazed lasciviously at the half cow steaming away. Its size caused it to slurp gravy into the next space where a cheesecake succumbed to the machinations of the hot gravy and subsided like a sailor's penis after a run ashore.

'Come back if you want any more boy!' The cook's red face beamed at me through the steam. All of the Yanks emanated friendship and hospitality beyond bounds. I felt at home!

We settled in the mess space. No conversation, just groans of pleasure as the steak juices dribbled from the corner of our mouths. We were joined by a group of off-duty Yankee crew, garrulous and friendly. Already a rapport was developing, which was not to fade as we explored the very different cultures we represented.

'The smoking lamp is lit . . . the smoking lamp is lit.' The Tannoy which for many moons was to rule our lives, boomed. The fans whirred as the Camels and Lucky Strikes were ignited. Contented sighs could be heard as we relaxed after the magnificent repast.

'If they are treating us like this, we must be on our way to a really shit job,' said a marine between contented belching.

Silence then as we realised the real purpose of our presence in the submarine.

'Sod it, let's enjoy it while we can.' The bubble of conversation re-started.

'Now hear this, now hear this . . . Royal Marines to their quarters'.

Our fat guide appeared, plump and breathless.'Come on guys, back to your bunks and settle in.'

We trundled back to the bow compartment and laid down on our bunks whilst the Yank matelots milled to and fro on their duties connected with the boat leaving harbour. The rumble of engine noises, the whirr of ventilating fans and the gentle sway in the compartment indicated that the boat was travelling slow ahead.

Following the gutbuster of a meal I had just demolished and with the gentle motion of the boat I felt my eyelids begin to droop. I was gazing at the grey painted steel bulkhead through half-closed eyes, and slowly darkness descended as I succumbed to the gentle blandishment of sleep. If one had to go to war, then there were definitely less comfortable ways to do so!

'Whooooosh' – I awoke with a start, aware that the motion of the boat was fairly smooth. The bunks were creaking, and remembering again the gravity route of spew, I metaphorically patted myself on the back again for my foresight in choosing a top bunk.

'Whooooosh' – At the noise I cast a startled look at the bunk opposite, where Lew Heard, one of my blokes, questioned the noise with a raised eyebrow.

'Whooooosh' of longer duration this time. I shrugged my shoulders at Lew – I didn't know what it was. The Tannoy called. 'Surface, surface'.

I then realised that the noise was compressed air forcing sea-water out of the ballast tanks and that, whilst my mates and I had slept, we had missed our first underwater sojourn and were regaining consciousness at the same time as the *Perch* was regaining the surface of the sea.

More training – we learned to clamber silently up ladders and out onto the upper deck at the maximum speed. Meanwhile the Yank crewmen had offloaded and inflated the rubber boats. Such was the efficiency that it was a rare occasion indeed when the boats were not bobbing alongside as we reached the deck. A tremendous mutual respect developed between the commandos and the submariners, each depending on, and aware of, the efficiency of the other.

As the commandos trained and worked together, an amazing esprit developed. I learned to trust my mates implicitly and had much respect for my immediate boss, Sergeant Sid Moon. He was a quiet and apparently gentle man who was an expert in the assault engineer field. Unlike the stereotype commando sergeant, I rarely heard him shout or rant, but the job always got done. I had, through experience, learned to hold Royal Navy officers in extreme contempt and agreed, without reservation, with the navy lower-deck terminology for them, 'The Pigs'. I admit reluctantly that their counterparts in the commando units, the Royal Marine officers, engendered in me a tremendous sense of loyalty as they, unlike their Naval counterparts, shared every discomfort and tribulation with the troops. In particular I admired the professional skill of 'Percy' Ovens though I would die rather than admit it loudly!

The pleasure of squatting in the rubber boats without paddling, whilst they, tied together bow to stern, tore across the surface of the sea being towed by the submarine at periscope depth, was unique. The boats were not designed for such rapid progress. Often, to our delight, after the sub had cast us adrift, miles out at sea, we could see the periscope describe an arc and pass between our boats to the accompaniment of loud cheers from the commandos, unheard, of course, by the Yankee crew, far below the surface. It was mentioned by the Captain that he had observed 'V'-signs through the periscope lenses as he passed the marines!

Almost the ultimate in man-management was when, on one occasion we paddled back to the '*Perch*', clambered silently aboard in our coral shoes and drifted back to our quarters in the bow torpedo area. We discovered that the Yanks had stowed away all of the tiers of bunks ... God knows where. We sat about comfortably in the unaccustomed space and were presented with steaming trays of yet more steak and ice cream. The submarine gently submerged as the crew rigged a cinema screen in our compartment and we were regaled with the latest Hollywood movies. I will always remember the overstated delight of the commandos as they cheered and whistled the large breasted ladies and heartily booed the villains as their shadows cavorted across the screen. Simple pleasures indeed, but bloody marvellous under the circumstances.

Then we were told to split into our respective groups.

'Gather round, men.' All over the boat space small groups of commandos were suddenly being briefed for what looked like, at last, the real thing. I squatted with the assault engineers, half a dozen of us, with Captain Ovens quietly putting us in the picture. No dramatics, just a serious chat. No flowery exhortations, but plain technical facts as to what was expected of us.

CHAPTER SIX

I Hear No Trains

I glanced around the small compartment. In spite of the presence of British understatement, there was drama in the air. The dim light revealed the serious faces of the marines, listening intently: no games now! I was conscious of a slightly unpleasant feeling in the pit of my stomach caused by the knowledge that what we were about to undertake, could result in death on a lonely beach, about a hundred miles behind the front line, in alien territory which was peopled by slant-eyed strangers who would not hesitate to do much mischief to prevent us completing our task. I had seen war films of landing from submarines, but there was no way they could indicate the tensions occasioned, nor the relief that, at last, we were up and going!

It evolved, through the briefing, that it was our intention to attack a railway tunnel which emerged near a beach and which was the main supply route to the south. We were to land, enter the tunnel and bury, about 50 yards in from the mouth, 300 pounds of explosives between the sleepers, with two pressure switches to be actuated by the arrival of the next train carrying stores and troops. The heavy charge was necessary to completely demolish the train inside the tunnel. One advantage the Koreans had was a propensity of manual labourers capable of clearing obstructions and damage very quickly. It would be singularly more difficult to sort the mess out inside a tunnel, and cause more casualties this way.

'We must be extremely cautious when first entering the tunnel,' said Percy, 'They tend to hide up, in their trains, inside the tunnels, to avoid air strikes . . . it may well be that a train could be waiting in there.'

I gulped, and once again looked around at the faces of my mates, some seemed a little pale in the artificial lighting of the submarine, but most looked fairly relaxed and ready to go. I was pleased, looking at them, that I was with them and not agin' them.

'Any questions?' said Percy, brightly oozing confidence.

I raised my arm tentatively. 'If, whilst laying the charge, a train comes hurtling through the tunnel, will there be sufficient time for us to get out?'

'I would think perhaps not,' smiled Percy. 'Just press yourselves against the walls of the tunnel, it's all very unlikely anyway.'

I thought that if the charges went off, I wouldn't need to press myself against the wall, I'd be pressed on the roof . . . in bits! I pondered on this dilemma, a 50-yard dash to the exit mouth, laden with equipment would probably take about 10 seconds or so. In that 10 seconds a train travelling at 60 miles per hour would cover about 300 yards... the odds didn't seem too rosy!

The one bright light on the horizon was, that as this was our first raid, our opposition would consist primarily of North Korean Home Guard types, a sort of slit-eyed Dad's Army!

Percy continued, 'The submarine will approach the shoreline and recce the beach from periscope depth this afternoon, then we will move out to sea a little, settle on the bottom and rest. We'll then come back in at about midnight and do the job, okay?'

The next few hours were spent sorting out the explosives and switches we would require for the raid. Military explosives are singularly easy to handle, paying, of course, the normal respect. They are not as delicate or unstable a substance as many laymen would presume. Providing one kept the detonators away from the main charge until required, then all would be well.

We oiled and cleaned our weapons with great care. I would welcome a misfire at the crucial moment with as much avidity as a prostitute would welcome syphilis! Both circumstances would be a serious impingement to our respective futures! The lads were quite noisy, the response to a perfectly mild humorous remark was hysterical laughter.

Percy wandered in. He was, in the circumstances, not always the harbinger of good tidings. 'If, for some reason or other you are unable to return to the boats and are left behind, frogmen will return to the beach and pick you up on the following night. If this is not successful, head for this peak here,' he stabbed his finger at a point on the aerial photograph, 'and we will attempt, the second day, to pick you up by helicopter,' he smiled comfortingly.

I returned the smile and, as my mind raced through the possible sequence of events, the smile slowly disappeared . . . if, whilst waiting, having been left behind, a troop train trundled over our booby trap, the surviving Korean soldiers would perhaps be a little upset with us! They would swarm over the surrounding countryside like avenging tigers. I figured the chances of escape would be fairly limited. There and then, I decided that should the shit hit the fan, and should I miss the boat, I would head south for about 100 miles to the welcoming arms of the UN forces. I figured that, with the impetus of fear, and if I could avoid skidding on my own excreta, it would, perhaps, take four or five days.

So to bed. I lay there in my bunk, my mind racing. The submarine was obviously at periscope depth, because a breathing device, a German invention called a 'Schnorkel', was supplying us with air through a tube alongside the periscope. Every time a wave passed over the valve, it closed to prevent the entry of water and, of course, air. This caused, on every stoppage, the eardrums to pop with the changing air pressure. My ears were popping away with the alacrity of an Irishman's bum after 12 pints of Guinness! I was very restless and would be happy when the first job was over.

The Tannoy system clicked. 'Now hear this . . . remain in your sacks. The boat will rest on the bottom . . . get some rest . . . do not move about, we wish to conserve oxygen.' We would be too deep to use the 'Schnorkel'.

The submarine creaked and groaned, a pleasant sound for a submariner but not too reassuring for a landlubber. A gentle lurch and all was still. We were stationary on the bottom of the sea. All was quiet, 60 commandos busy with their own thoughts, one or two already snoring!

Click! 'That blasted tannoy again,' I thought, mildly irritated.

'Royal Marines, the smoking lamp is lit . . . the smoking lamp is lit.' Click.

'What is he talking about?' I thought, 'Here we are, lying quietly, conserving oxygen, and some pratt is saying that it is okay to have a cigarette!'

Oh well. I reached for my cigarettes and matches. After an unbelieving pause from the others I could hear the rattle of matches and the click of lighters resounding through the quiet compartment. Puzzled but pleased, I positioned a cigarette between my lips and struck a match. For one brief moment the head of the match glowed. It immediately went out! I tried another with exactly the same result. All through the troop space lighters were clicking to no avail and matches were extinguishing themselves.

'The bastards are taking the piss!' came a gruff exclamation from a nearby bunk. This opinion was reinforced when a gentle chuckle boomed from the tannoy loudspeaker. We had all been well and truly had over. The oxygen content in the air was insufficient to maintain the required ignition from the matches. I felt like a young apprentice who had been sent on an errand for a left-handed spanner . . . a right bloody idiot!

'Wakey, wakey! Let go of your cocks and grab your socks!' The time-honoured method of waking sleeping marines was being called. I stirred and opened my eyes. The normal lighting had been extinguished and in its place the illumination was deep red. This was deliberately done because with such lighting the eyes don't have to adjust to the sudden onslaught of darkness outside, they are prefocused by the red glow. The sub was obviously in motion. Memory flooded back from the deep sleep which had encompassed me in merciful oblivion. It all came back in a flash. The submarine, the intended landing . . . the lot. My mind raced. I preferred the solace of deep sleep. I clambered down from my bunk and was soon kitted up with the bare essentials. A green waterproof combat suit, a webbing belt from which hung a water bottle, a knife, a first aid pouch and entrenching tool. In a loop around my neck was a canvas container holding 50 rounds of ammunition. On my head, a green beret minus identification badge. Finally, with a grunt, I heaved three packages over my shoulder, each containing 20 pounds of plastic explosive. With the weight of my weapon, the combined load would ensure that, in the event of my falling into the sea, I would swim like a bastard to no avail because I would head for the bottom, fast. I padded around in my quiet canvas shoes – no noise – softly, softly, and positioned myself in the queue around a ladder leading upwards to a hatch which was our exit to the upper deck. Whilst waiting these few minutes, there was no conversation, a thumbs-up to one mate, a raised eyebrow to another. Our blackened faces enhanced the whiteness of the eyes and teeth. I was surprised in these moments of heightened awareness as to how white and gleaming teeth are against a black background. I resolved, if possible, whilst ashore, in the interest of camouflage, not to smile too much! I smiled at the thought.

'Whoooooosh' roared the compressed air as the sub began to surface. 'Sh . . . I thought, be quiet you noisy bastard . . . for Christ's sake ahhh!'

'Whoooooosh' again.

I could imagine all the Korean soldiers ashore jerking their heads in the direction of the noise, nudging one another and saying, 'Get leddy, they have allived,' or the Korean equivalent.

I was unhappy about all that noise.

'Surface . . . surface.'

I could hear the thumping and banging as the clambering Yanks on the upper deck unloaded and prepared our boats.

With a loud clang the hatch above was opened. There was a blast of warm fresh beautiful air and bright moonlight flooded into the submarine.

'Shit . . . the moon's out.'

No time to sit and think, we quickly leapt up the ladder and out onto the slippery upper deck, awash as the sub was barely above the surface of the sea. The fresh air smelt fragrant and the night was warm and cloudless. There, bobbing alongside were, our mobile torture chambers, each rubber boat being held against the side of the sub by two Yank matelots. We climbed aboard with practised ease and faster than we had ever done in training, across the bulging sponsons of the submarine and settled on the rubber gunwales. I reached down and grabbed a wooden paddle, my palms slightly sweating.

'So long. Good luck fellahs', whispered a submariner as he threw the bowline into the boat. He scampered away and, with his mates, rapidly disappeared through the hatch and into the boat. The submarine slowly drew apart from us and disappeared into the night. We were alone.

One advantage that paddling had over conventional rowing is that you are facing the direction of travel, therefore at least you can see where you are going. The tension was such that every detail was revealed in stark clarity as we peered into the night. The view, under different circumstances, would have been considered beautiful. The sea was a gentle swell with illuminating fluorescence glowing at every disturbance of the smooth surface. In the distance the dark outline of the coastline with its succession of humps, peculiar to Korean landscape, produced a bluish tinge in the moonlight. To an artist the coastline was perfection; to a paddling marine, searching anxiously for the first sign of gleaming tracer bullets, it was singularly ominous.

I could see that, as taught, our five boats were in line abreast with the marines crouched over the sides of the boats like jockeys, the flashing paddles the only movement and the disturbance they were causing producing a gleaming pointer to our presence. We kept carefully in line abreast. No boat race this! No urge to win! One boat landing well before the others would be a prime target; there was a survival percentage in arriving together.

As we slogged silently towards the shore we were all deep in our own respective thoughts. I was remembering and blessing the constant training which was enabling us to build up speed to get ashore as quickly as we bloody well could! This was the moment of great danger, we were, should things go amiss, sitting ducks. I touched my gun, briefly, to reassure myself that it was still there. I have heard, many times, people of pacifist mentality state that they could never shoot at anyone with intent to kill. I would willingly bet anyone a pound to a pinch of shit, that, under these circumstances, they definitely would! When one's life is on the line, ethics fly very rapidly out of the window.

As we drew closer I could hear the gentle splash as the surf creamed onto the beach. All eyes were now on the higher ground beyond the beach. Each darkly outlined bush became a prospective Korean, eager to cancel us out before we had started. I could understand how ill-disciplined troops fired wildly in all directions at moments of doubt. I swallowed my concern, even though I was sure that the dark mound, on the oncoming beach, the target of my anxious eye, had just moved!

Not a word from the boats, the beauty of the scenery long forgotten and drowned in a wave of uncertainty. Imagination caused the skyline to appear heavily populated with moving Koreans. Their silhouettes bearing a strong similarity to bushes . . . or were they? My eyes must have been protruding like organ stops!

'Stand by to beach!' came a whisper from the bow.

I immediately stopped paddling and as the bows grated over the coarse sand I dropped my paddle and leapt ashore. Flitting shadows to my left and right melted into the darkness as the marines quietly dispersed, to search for and destroy, as quietly as possible, any lurking oriental soldiery.

I approached, cautiously, the dark mound which had been the focus of my attention on the way in. A sigh of relief as it revealed itself to be a largish rock protruding from the sand. Complete concentration on my own task now. I crept forward through the night. A slight rise and there it was, a shining ribbon of railway line, it's gleam indicating that it was frequently used. With my mates I turned left and walked along the railway sleepers. I do not know who designated the distance apart railway sleepers should be, but, invariably they are too close together for one step, and if you decide to walk stepping on alternate sleepers, they are too far apart. This phenomenon is as true in the Orient as it is in Europe. So we stumbled on until ahead we could see a slightly darker patch than the surrounding night . . . the tunnel entrance. It would be a complete understatement to describe our entry into the dark abyss as ultra-cautious. No ballet dancer has ever tiptoed so lightly. The slightest unusual noise and I am sure we would all *'pas de deuxed'* right back to the beach!!

We stopped ... listened ... silence, as we counted our way 50 yards into the tunnel. Again, stop and listen. I measured the distance from the line to the tunnel wall. The tunnel had been dug with economy in mind and there was not a lot of spare room. Definitely, I decided, the emergence of an unexpected train would have to be responded to by wild flight! Squeezing against the wall was a definite non-event in the survival stakes.

We scooped the clinker and soil away from between two of the sleepers, gathered together the 15 explosive packs, joined the detonating cords from each so that they were enmeshed like a daisy-chain, only slightly more lethal. We carefully placed the packs in position in the aperture we had made, covered the charges with clinker and attached the prepared switches

It was going quite nicely ... the only noise was the chirp of tropical insects which are a feature of warmer climes. The switches were positioned and the first safety pins removed. The delicate operation of removing the second pins and all would be done. Then, without warning, from the depths of the tunnel I could hear the shuffle of feet across shingle and the high pitched jabber of oriental chatter. The sounds were close, very close, and there were obviously a fair number of them.

Crack ... crack ... the sound of two shots from nearby and the sparking star of a ricochet glanced off the tunnel wall. In the brief flash of light I saw that one of the marines had fired. There was a scream from deep in the tunnel and the sound of lots of pairs of feet scampering away. There was no return fire. We squatted silently for a few seconds. Then, in the distance, the heart-stopping sound of a train!

'Shit and derision!' I may have been last away, but I was

definitely first to emerge from the tunnel, going like a long dog! We threw ourselves to the ground and took up firing positions.

'What's up?' asked a quiet voice from the darkness.

'It's a fucking train,' I recognised the quaking voice as mine.

'I can't hear a train,' another voice, 'No.'

I listened intently. Not a sound: if it had been a train it would have been with us by now.

We clambered shamefacedly to our feet. Gentle laughter poured from the surrounding darkness. I was never allowed to forget the incident. No matter how much we in the tunnel at the time protested that we had heard it, our pleas fell on deaf ears. The unit Christmas card on the following Christmas displayed me hurtling from the mouth of the tunnel as its main theme.

I glanced down at my hand, there, reposing innocently, was the second safety pin. I had obviously wrenched it out with wild abandon before having it away on my toes. Carefully we retraced our steps into the tunnel. Everyone was anxious to leave fairly soon because of the Koreans we had fired at. They would be keen to impart their knowledge of our presence, at the earliest opportunity, to their own side. However, our journey back was necessary to ensure that all was well with the charges and switches abandoned in our hasty flight from the ghost train! All was well. We crept back and, at the designated time, commenced our withdrawal to the beach. The boats were there, a welcome sight! We clambered aboard and started paddling. No keeping in line now, it had indeed become a boat race! When about a hundred yards out to sea we suddenly felt like sitting ducks, in spite of the darkness, for, from the dark hills we had left behind, 'tack, tack, tack, tack', a long burst from what was obviously a heavy machine gun.

Fortunately it was not firing tracer bullets, so not only could he not see where his shot was falling, we could not see either, which was good news. Wherever he was firing, nothing came close to us, but it did increase the rate of paddling to a hitherto unbelievable rate. If Oxford or Cambridge boat crews had the same circumstances with a machine gun firing behind them, they would do Putney to Mortlake in one minute flat, and we would have overtaken them with no bother at all. The unsporting Koreans in the tunnel must have grassed to their army who had arrived just a fraction too late.

Whilst still paddling, but by now a little less frantically, there was a muffled boom from the mainland... it sounded as though our charges may have done their stuff, but we weren't going to go back and see, so we will never know!

As we drew further to seawards and the tension lifted, we relaxed and chatted together. The main discussion was about the mythical train, with considerable mickey taking. I decided to get my own back, immediately. As we paddled along I remembered that the rubber boats had compartmentalised air bags, and would sink if all were punctured. I pursed by lips together and made a loud hissing sound. At once the banter stopped as everyone aboard listened anxiously. I stopped hissing, immediately the paddling recommenced. After a while I hissed loud and long again. Again and anxious silence, I was thoroughly enjoying myself. Suddenly I burst as a paddle hit me in the small of my back.

'You bastard, you bastard... it's Brady making that noise.'

I roared, but strangely none of the marines seemed to see the funny side of it all!

We stopped paddling and the boats gathered together in the smooth sea a couple of miles off shore. From the lead boat a strange contraption was hoist aloft. It was the broom handle with the biscuit tin appended to the end. I discovered afterwards that we were so low in the water that the submarine radar couldn't pick up our position, but it could locate the biscuit tin held high in the air. So much for the miracles of modern science.

Then out of the darkness loomed our old mate USS *Perch*. What a welcome sight, because we would have been fairly substantially in the tripe if it had not turned up. As the boat approached we let out an involuntary cheer which was reciprocated by the Yank crewmen on deck.

'Any casualties?' came a shout from the deck.

'No.'

The Yank medics turned away and scampered below taking their unnecessary stretchers with them. It dawned upon me that the operation really had gone according to plan. Had I known that this would be one of the few occasions when such good fortune would occur, I should have perhaps appreciated it more, as it was we were full of high spirits and delighted with our night's work. On occasions such as this, one never thinks of the pain and suffering that one is responsible for. I never, for instance, dwelt upon the carnage that would, and maybe already had, occurred, on the actuation of the explosives we had laid. It was war. They would do the same to us if they could. The only winners really were the ambitious politicians who had made it all necessary. The bastards!

All in all, we had had a fairly successful baptism. Our confidence was high and our morale could not have been greater. As we clambered aboard the sub the uneasy qualms in my stomach settled once again. The only discomfort was the realisation that, in comparison with the beautiful night air, the interior of the sub smelled like a Turkish wrestler's jockstrap. The hatches clanged shut and the boat vibrated as we quietly crept away from the inhospitable shore.

Joy, however, was short lived . . . Percy appeared. 'We are to do another job tonight, men.' He was businesslike and exuded confidence.

CHAPTER SEVEN

I'll Never Eat Rice Again

'Aerial photographs will be delivered at noon today and we will plan accordingly.' We settled in to shipboard routine. The troop area was in a 'lights out' situation, emulating night to ensure that we enjoyed a good long sleep before the labours to come in a few hours. Once again I dozed in my bunk, a little restlessly in view of what I imagined was to come.

Some hours later the 'chow down' broadcast caused my disembarkation from the haven of my bunk. There was never enough room and the constant jostling for space, would, I was certain, cause problems if it were to continue for many more days. After a liberal helping of frankfurters and beans, waffles and syrup and copious cups of superb coffee, it was time to have a little chat with Percy.

As we gazed at the photographs, airdropped to us a few short hours ago whilst we were deep in slumber, I groaned inwardly. There was our target, a railway embankment with a convenient culvert in which to lay our charges. I groaned because I realised at once that we would be using an explosive called Amatol for this type of demolition. Whilst our normal high explosive was supplied in 20-pound packs, amatol was packed in 80-pound canisters, awkward and heavy to manipulate. We would need a fair amount of explosive to lift and distribute the embankment over a wide area, all of which would have to be manhandled into the boats and also carried ashore. The one satisfying feature would be that we would explode the stuff and see it do its stuff, rather than sneak away and be unable to observe the fruits of our labour.

American naval vessels are 'dry' in that they are alcohol free. This was sad. However, they do carry small quantities of 'medicinal brandy' and it was therefore somewhat of a pleasant surprise, when, whilst loitering, bathed in the red pre-embarkation lights, to find, thrust into one's grubby little hand, a miniature bottle of 'medicine'. I swigged mine immediately, delicious, a few more of those and I would be able to manage the forthcoming operation alone!

With the confidence engendered by the success of the night before there was little pre-battle anxiety, apart from the gentle gnawing sensation at the pit of the stomach; I think it's called, in enlightened society, fear!

The loading of the heavy canisters into the bobbing boats took a little longer than usual. Again the moon was shining brightly and the air was sheer nectar. I reflected that this was an infinitely preferable method of waging war than skulking in a foxhole for days on end, in intense discomfort, with hordes of foreigners aiming lethal objects in one's direction. With a sharp obscenity and a grunt I deposited an 80-pound canister into the rubber boat. It settled a little lower in the sea. It would be a bastard to paddle.

Once again we were off, as before, in line abreast as we approached the threatening shoreline. The same bushes became the same non-existent Korean soldiers. The gentle persuasion of the recently imbibed 'medicine' eased the tension, what a good idea that had been!

The accompanying marines melted away as we landed. I followed Percy to a huge embankment. I became aware of the most vile smell. I sniffed it and analysed it rapidly. There was no doubt in my mind at all, it was definitely excreta. Not only did my wrinkled nostrils recognise it as such, but, by rolling it around as though it were a particularly good vintage wine, my taste buds established that the effluence was human. It couldn't be Percy, he was definitely not short of bottle. Could it be me? I investigated, no, it wasn't me! The dark hole of the culvert hove into view.

'Here we are,' whispered Percy. If he could smell what I could, he was too much of a gentleman to mention it. I only hoped that he did not presume that I was the source.

'Get in there and place the charges, I have chaps coming from the other side, they will lay sandbags back from the charges. Your men can sandbag back from this side. Any questions?'

As he spoke, the smell became almost overpowering, I followed my nose and discovered that the smell was from the culvert. I could hear a gurgling noise as a fluid gently oozed from within. Percy quickly hurried away and I didn't blame him. I knelt by the entrance to the culvert which was about four feet in diameter. A foul-smelling slurry about a foot deep trickled from the aperture in a channel that had been produced by wear over many years. It was horrible. A tentative probe with my knife proved that though the surface few inches were fluid and mobile, a thick residue had coagulated beneath the surface and was of awe-inspiring consistency and power. I turned to my blokes. 'Right oh lads, in you go. One can of amatol each, one at a time, hurry on lads.'

I stood back a little and pointed, emulating Percy. Not one of them moved! Chaka's Zulu Impis were willing to throw themselves over a precipice to prove their discipline to the death, but my miserable bastards blanched at the mere 12 inches of shit! I pondered. Where had the human crap come from anyway? Then I remembered that in our lectures about Korea and the Koreans, we had been told that the natives fertilised their rice paddies with human excreta. This culvert had probably been in use for over 50 years carrying away the residue from the fields ... 'I'll never eat rice again,' I thought.

'Come on lads,' I whispered, slightly more aggressively on this, the second exhortation.

A shadow loomed out of the darkness. I removed my weapon from under his nose when I realised that Percy had returned.

'Get in there, Corporal. We haven't all bloody day,' he seemed cross! He lingered and pointed, looking me straight in the eye. He showed no sign of disappearing. He was Chaka, I became the Impi, so I took a deep obnoxious breath and leapt into the evil quagmire. It squelched beneath my feet, the hard underlying crust held my weight for a brief moment and then cracked as I gently settled into the disgusting substance. It overflowed and crept into the top of my coral shoes. I heard glugs and gasps as the rest of the Impi joined me!

Percy wandered off to supervise in slightly more salubrious surroundings. I crouched into the abyss pushing an 80-pound can of Amatol before me. Guessing 15 feet I stopped and positioned the explosive. In the confined space the methane content became ghastly. I was unhappy! Ahead of me I could hear the 'phews' of the other half of the team positioning the sandbags. Can after can was passed through which I carefully stacked. I crawled backwards out of the culvert and was pleased to see the lads crawling back in dragging sandbags which were being filled by other marines. I had unrolled the detonating cord and in a short while the task was completed. So horrendous was the Korean excrement that all fear of enemy activity was washed from my mind. Percy appeared with the necessary implements to detonate the charge. The stuff ceased to flow and bubble from the now sandbagged culvert. I could almost imagine the nauseous build-up inside. The smell, however, grew no less because we were liberally daubed in it. This became obvious as we crept back to the beach because other marines, on the same route, veered away violently on approaching us, whispering marine-type endearments regarding the aroma emanating from our soiled clothing.

The welcome sight of the boats dispelled my misgivings about the state of nausea engendered by the Korean excrement clinging to my clothing. We climbed aboard as we pushed the boat out to sea. The fluorescent sea had scoured the worst obscenity from my uniform. We settled in for the usual paddle, after Percy, the last man ashore, had rejoined us after having initiated the time delay on the explosive charges we had laid. As the shore faded from view the time grew near for the demolition to activate. So, as practised on many an occasion, we stopped and paddled the boats about so that we were facing the beach. It is a fact that when a large explosion takes place, and if you are a reasonable distance from it, it is safer to stand and look up than to lay down flat, with your face buried in trembling arms. By looking up it is possible to avoid the large slow-moving chunks of debris as they fall to earth, or, in this case, to sea! The boats could be manoeuvred, with frantic paddling to ensure the safety of the occupants. A large chunk of railway embankment, landing in the middle of a frail rubber boat could cause it to sink with disconcerting rapidity. Discipline is essential. Because the boat's crew had to obey any order immediately, there was no future in one half paddling one way and the other half in the opposite direction. Under such circumstances the boat would not move at all, thus presenting a stationary target for the large lump of Korean masonry cascading towards it.

'Look up!' shouted Percy.

'Whooff'. A tremendous explosion completely destroyed the railway embankment. The chunks of debris did indeed soar into the air, arching towards us. However, less dangerous but considerably more insidious, was the fact that the culvert, immediately prior to its destruction, had acted like a rifle barrel, but, instead of firing bullets it propelled, seawards, copious quantities of rapid flying Korean crap! Most of it dissipated as it lost momentum through the night air, but sufficient retained its flow in enough volume to settle gently on our recently sea-washed uniforms. The now familiar fragrance re-established itself. However, we were not alone: the whole raiding party now had their share, we were no longer pariahs!

The broom handle and biscuit tin were hoist aloft, invisibly informing the Perch of our stinking location. Half an hour later, sure enough, the grey submarine emerged from the darkness. We quickly drew alongside.

'Goddam . . . what's that fuckin' smell?' The Yankee crewmen drew back appalled.

We scrambled past them and scuttled below. It had been impressed upon us, from the beginning, that it was 'infra dig' to loiter on the upper deck of the sub at any time. Therefore, without any explanation, and irrespective as to the smell we were introducing to the boat, we raced through the hatch and down below. As Billy Connelly once said, we were as welcome as a fart in a space suit! The Yanks are a very hygienic race and were physically offended by the pong. But not half as offended as I was, when I realised that some of them presumed that we had had a difficult time and the cause of the excreta smell was our own, produced through terror. Cheeky bastards!

We were aware that, whilst we were paddling ashore and demolishing the railway system, to the annoyance of the North Koreans, that two other sections of the commando were performing the same function against the same railway system, from two Yankee assault personnel destroyers, the *'Wantuck'* and *'Bass'* which would obviously, in time, cause the foe to post regular troops along the coastline instead of the inept local forces they had been using to date. This also was part of the reason for our escapades, if we could not only disrupt their supply line, but also cause them to deploy troops from the front line, then we were at least accomplishing something!

The submarine landings could obviously not continue much longer. There were two reasons, one was the approaching winter. It was extremely cold in the winter months at the latitude in which we were operating and the type of craft we were using were not suitable for deep cold operations. The second reason was the rapid advance of the United Nations forces. The amount of coastline to be attacked was diminishing at a pleasing rate and soon there would be little left for us to do in this sphere. For that reason we were informed that there was just one to go and then we would hoof it back to the fleshpots of Japan, not forgetting the married quarters of the Seventh Cavalry!

The usual briefing and then, hopefully, for the last time, with my mates, we gathered around the ladder leading to the upper deck to await the clanging of the hatch as the submarine surfaced. In the dim red illumination I glanced around at them. It occurred to me that the picture they produced was fairly dramatic, with faces blackened and bristling with firearms and assorted paraphernalia of war. They looked, and were, proficient and tough. I wanted to remember the sight so that I could bore the arse off my grandchildren in the years to come, with vivid descriptions of the occasion. Alas, I wouldn't do so, for fear of being considered a bullshitter, until now. Still, I was part of history and, should I survive, would be mildly proud.

As we paddled towards the now familiar shoreline I felt no more than the normal slight sense of apprehension. I had become blasé because of the unmitigated success we had had so far. Peering through the darkness, over the shoulder of the marine ahead, I searched frantically for any sign of movement: nothing. The usual darker lumps which in the earlier raids would have caused me mild apoplexy were brushed aside as bushes or rocks. When we were about twenty yards from the beach-line it happened! A few sparkling lights flickered from the shore, followed a short time afterwards by the crackle of small-arms fire. I realised, with a sudden shock that all was not well when I noted that not only was I very wet, but that I was swimming like mad, and sinking like a stone, weighed down by the heavy explosives packs slung over my shoulder. My bottle was going at a rapid rate. Commonsense told me that I should shed the load I was carrying, but survival instinct would not allow my arms to stop flailing about in a swimming motion. Had I had time to assess the situation calmly I would perhaps have admitted that I was probably drowning.

With some surprise I felt my body rising to the surface. I had just run out of breath and was swallowing gallons of salty Korean sea water. As my face broke the surface I found myself dangling at the end of a huge muscular arm, beyond which was a familiar grinning face. 'What are you doing, you silly bastard?'

The angel of mercy was the frogman, Rex Swancott. He was a huge powerful man and I was dangling from his arm like a pike on the end of a fisherman's hook. I spluttered and spat, unable to reply, grateful and relieved, with water pouring from every aperture of my body. He pulled me towards the shore until finally my feet touched terra firma. He released his grip and disappeared up the beach. I never did thank him subsequently, but he knew!

Some 40 years later I obtained Rex Swancott's address and wrote him a letter stating, 'As I am now retired and in my dotage, I have expenses which would not have accrued if you had not saved my life many years ago in Korea. Therefore, I feel it is your duty to send mew a monetary contribution, because had you, those many years ago, let me die, I would not have had to subsist my continuence.' I received a reply much to obvious too be quoted here plus a 50-yen banknote from the 1950s, worth about five pence.

Now that the trauma of my involuntary swim faded I became aware of the situation on the beach. It was quite dark with not much moon but there was sufficient light to distinguish the dark shapes of the marines, prone on the beach. Tracer was arching towards us. The main position of the enemy appeared to be around the mouth of the tunnel, which was our intended target. The situation had developed into somewhat of a problem. We would have to dispose of the Koreans fairly rapidly, because, without a doubt, there would be reinforcements on the way. We would not regain our boats and paddle away whilst under fire, the boats being too fragile and easily sunk. It was necessary to render the Koreans *hors de combat*.

I wriggled myself deeper into the soft sand of the beach. There was shadowy movement near the mouth of the tunnel. I fired a short burst, as did some of my mates, and the figure crumpled to the ground. The orientals were not as inscrutable as we had been led to believe, for, as two or three grenades exploded near their position I could clearly hear the sing-song intonations of the Korean language. The words clearly indicated that there was a certain amount of panic going on over there! As another grenade arched through the air, the jabbering became louder, with not a word being spoken by the commando troops. The grenade exploded, to be immediately followed by a shout from one of the marines, who followed the grenade in, firing long bursts as he did so. Then silence, apart from the pattering feet disappearing into the tunnel and away. The Koreans had had it away on their toes.

It is amazing how acute one's hearing becomes under moments of stress. In the ensuing silence we listened, oh, how we listened! There was the sound of considerable movement inland, indicating that the Koreans would soon be with us in strength. A clandestine element is lost. This coupled with the fragility of our modes of transport, the rubber boats, caused me to feel that it would probably be a good idea to shove off when the time was right. As the coward in me asserted itself I felt sincerely that the right time was now! I turned my head to the dark figure prone on the beach beside me, unrecognisable in the deep night light,

'If I was Duggie, I think I would piss off now, wouldn't you?' I whispered.

'Well, you are not, I am, and we will!' To my immense surprise the voice was that of Duggie Drysdale, our colonel. I could see his teeth gleam as he smiled. The orders passed along the line, and with as much dignity as we could muster under the circumstances, we crept back to our boats. We quietly paddled away in complete silence and not before time, because, as we hoisted the biscuit tin, a terrific fire fight started ashore. It lasted for so long that the considered opinion of the marines was that two Korean contingents had met in the dark and were tremendously busy annihilating one another. As their tracers arched on the shoreline my rectum resumed its normal shape . . . our luck had held yet again. As we settled in the cramped sweaty confines of the submarine our spirits were high. The engines pulsing and thrusting the submarines bows towards Japan, back to Camp McGill, back to the Ginza, to Asahi beer and the Seventh Cavalry's married quarters, the only complaint was that the engines were not thrusting quite fast enough.

During the long journey we were allowed, in groups of three, to climb up to the conning tower for a breath of fresh air for a minute or two. When my turn came, I climbed through the hatch and out onto the bridge. The sea air was bloody marvellous. There was little conversation. The Yankee lookouts were peering anxiously through their powerful binoculars and scanning the empty horizon with the officer-of-the-watch busy, watching! I revelled in the scene, it epitomised the glamour of warfare, or at least the Hollywood substitute for the real thing . . . here was drama without danger. The sea spilling over the bows of the boat, the lean hard-looking men peering over the apron of the conning tower, it was all there. The horizon was clear as far as the eye could see and all was well with the world. I was aware that as we were travelling south towards Japan, that to the west of us millions of men were engaged in combat and dying. Suddenly I felt a little guilty at my complacency and climbed back into the submarine feeling that the discomfort below decks would perhaps assuage my guilt to a small degree. It didn't!

Our rapport with the crew of the *Perch* grew. We were aware that once we had disembarked it would be goodbye until next summer, if the war lasted that long. We enjoyed, once more, a fim show below decks, and made arrangements for a good booze-up with the crew, on our return to Nippon. We would miss, most of all, the magnificent grub, because without doubt the American submarine service fed their men with more and better food than any other armed service in the world. Whilst we were with them we shared their good fortune, but did not envy them their claustrophobic existence. At least, in our occupation we could make individual decisions which would affect our survival, they had little choice in their steel tomb, and were welcome to it!

CHAPTER EIGHT

New Shoes

At last, back in Camp McGill, heaven. All the space we required, one could fart with impunity aware that the aroma would not linger in a confined space and cause one instant and vindictive unpopularity. We had decided that we would savour the delights of a Japanese sukiyaki meal in genuine Japanese surroundings and so, with light hearts and heavy wallets from accrued and unspent pay, we headed for the delights of Tokyo. After a few ales, about twenty of us, in assorted conditions, depending on our ability to assimilate the joys of Asahi beer, settled into the distinctly Japanese surrounding of a Sukiyaki house. The alleged geishas present indicated that it was fairly genuine, but the long corridors of assorted rooms adjacent to the banqueting room hinted geishas were not genuine, because the true Geisha may be many things, but a prostitute she very rarely is, according to the Geisha code.

The first offering, whilst we squatted on cushions around the low table, were small handleless cups of warm clear liquid, saki. It tasted innocuous and I downed a good few. They are not daft, these Japanese, they were only too aware that the greatest propensity produced by saki, particularly to the long-nosed foreigners, was brewer's droop! The food arrived in large pitchers which were placed, on mobile heaters in the centre of the table. The bowls of steaming rice were obviously to be supplemented by handfuls of the gloriously smelling pitchers. Above the table, hanging from the ceiling, was a delightful chandelier, which was, later on, to play the main part in disrupting an otherwise pleasant evening. The geishas grew more attractive as the saki swam potently down our gullet, to join with the unaccustomed food, which was already attacking our digestive systems with devastating effect.

The marines grew more boisterous and the geishas in some danger as the meal progressed. The manager, a large heavy-built man, smiled with his lips, but not with his eyes, as he realised that the booking he had welcomed, with open arms, was perhaps not progressing as sanguinely as he had anticipated. He was, however, not too unhappy, having insisted on payment prior to the commencement of the night's activities. The oriental ladies present, now that the marines were sated with food and booze, began to negotiate the cost, with their prospective customers, of the one hunger as yet unsatisfied. All was going well with the boisterousness more or less controlled. I was slumped on my cushion with my vision dimmed, peering through lowered lids at the tabletop, which appeared to be undulating. I peered at the lady sitting beside me. God, she was ugly! I tried to imagine what she would look like to a sober marine, because ugliness in a woman is an attribute, which rapidly disappears when one is in one's cups.

'Two thousand yen?' the beast whispered in my ear.

Fortunately for me the decision was taken from me. It happened!

A particularly large marine suddenly stood up, swayed a little, beat his chest with his fists like a demented gorilla and opened his mouth wide. 'AH-ey-ah-ey-aaaaaaaaaaah,' he roared. As the dying notes of his Tarzan-like incantation beat upon my eardrums, he leapt, arms outstretched, across the table and swung from the chandelier. He completed one swing to the cheers of the drunken marines, but, as he pendulumed and was situated above the large pitchers of food, the entire structure broke free from the ceiling, and in a shower of wood and straw he landed with a tremendous crash among the shattered debris he had caused. The mess was indescribable.

'Go get MPs,' I heard the manager, somewhat agitated, call to a Japanese man who scurried rapidly from the premises. Remembering my previous fracas with the MPs and recalling their accuracy with their clubs, I felt that it was probably the time to have it away on my toes. Duggie wouldn't be too amused if I were to have to meet him again under the aftermath of alleged violence. I staggered to my feet. From adjoining rooms various marines appeared, minus assorted items of clothing. Time to go!

As we poured from the building into the narrow back streets of Tokyo, we scattered in all directions, having grabbed the nearest pair of shoes, which were lined at the entrance inner door. I had at least shown a little profit, for the shoes I had picked up were of much better quality than my own, and they fitted! The unlucky marines that night were those who had just paid for their desires, and whom, their hunger unrequited, had grabbed, in their flight, a pair of shoes the wrong size.

The following morning, after negotiation with the unfortunate marine who had organised the event, and was therefore the only one who could be traced by the authorities, we had a whipround to pay for the damage we had caused. Payment was made to the restaurant owner and no more was heard. Shoes passed from hand to hand as the original owners attempted to regain their property. However, to my shame, I retained the luxurious pair I had grabbed, so I did show a little profit on the disastrous evening.

Training continued, I should have been mildly suspicious, because none of it had a nautical bent. Whatever plans were in store for us it was fairly obvious that our autonomy as a small raiding unit was soon to be a thing of the past, for the time being at least. We refreshed our knowledge of mines and booby traps and little emphasis was put on the use of explosives, it looked as though, now that November was here, that raiding was kaput until the following summer. I had hoped that we would be allowed to languish in the fleshpots of Japan, but that hypothesis didn't seem likely.

CHAPTER NINE

Goodbye McGill

Each morning, whilst at Camp McGill, our day started with a unit parade. It is definitely a misconception held by the layman, that commando troops, because of the nature of their work, are mercenaries who, whilst adept at warfare, are not too hot on normal military ceremony and discipline. This is not so. The unit parade was intended to reinforce the fact that we were Royal Marines, and the standard of appearance and drill was as high as one would expect at a marines establishment in the UK. The parade used to draw an audience of Yankee soldiers each morning. Because the American army, with its other faults, was fairly weak on both discipline and drill. We played hard when off duty, but we were under the control of our seniors when at work!

At the culmination of the parade one particular morning, with a deep chill in the air, it being mid-November, 1950, instead of the customary shouted order of, 'Dismiss!' we were marched from the parade and halted outside the quartermaster's store. We had been training hard and were as fit and fast as a fiddler's elbow. No rubber boats this time. The news from the front had been good, the North Koreans appeared to be in full flight. General MacArthur, the supreme ego in the Far East, had proclaimed, 'Home for Christmas', to his victorious soldiers, who were well into North Korea at this time. Such was his optimism that we were anxious to go rather than miss the back end of the war.

A huge bundle of clothing was issued to each marine. I staggered back to my barrack room and dumped the gear on my bed. There was a bulky fur-lined outer coat, with a hood, called a parka. It looked expensive and I wondered how many bottles of Asahi the selling price would purchase if the end came too soon. Pairs of woollen long john underpants, thick heavy socks, a huge pair of rubber outer boots called 'ShoesPacks', scarves, jumpers and balaclava helmets completed the inventory. If Scott had been as well equipped he would have survived his snowy terror, I am sure! With all the bulky clothing donned and our accoutrements strung about us we were transformed, like American football players, from fairly healthy-sized specimens to gigantic monsters incapable of rapid movement. Later the same day the unit was assembled in the mess hall, sitting about, smoking and endeavouring to sort the wheat from the chaff in the rumours that abounded. What was for sure was that we were on our way to North Korea, but in what capacity? We were much too lightly armed for a line unit's responsibilities; we had no transport of our own except a few Jeeps, which meant that we were fairly short on the ground in our supply of trained drivers. We had been trained, through our service, to act as a small independent force, what had they in mind for us? We were about to discover.

'Attention!' roared 'Sticky' Baines, his voice pervading into every crevasse causing the commandos to leap to attention like bleeding robots!

All the bossmen trooped in. I spotted my governor, Captain Ovens; his expression gave nothing away. He was as impassive as a Scotsman about to be lumbered into buying a round. I looked at these men who held my fate in their hands. Generally I have little respect for people who, by an accident of birth, aspire to lead their lessers! For once the corps had seemed to have got it right. 'Duggie' Drysdale led the way, closely followed by the second in command, Major Aldridge, a large powerful man with a granite face which belied his tremendous sense of humour. He was looking about and grinning, whatever we were to be told, at least he was pleased!

'Break ranks,' called 'Duggie'.

We closed round him and listened agog for the news he was about to impart. After all, it was relatively important to us!

'Till now, we have been under the command of Admiral Joy's raiding forces. As from now that has all changed, we are, as of this time now under the command of the 1st Division, The United States Marine Corps.' A buzz of interested conversation passed through the assembled commando. This meant that we were not going to be under the control of the Commonwealth Division in Korea, but were going back to north-east Korea, our old hunting ground, but, of course, much further inland. Duggie continued as the babble of noise settled down. There were about 180 commandos present, the entire unit, but you could hear a pin drop as the Intelligence Sergeant unfolded a large map of Korea which he draped over a blackboard.

'We will be moving from here tomorrow traveling by sea to Hungnam, which is a few miles south of the area we have been attacking from the sea. At Hungnam we will collect transport and US Marine transport drivers, and they will convey us to the area of the Chosin Reservoir, just south of the Manchurian border. This is the present limit of the advance. This area is sparsely populated and very, very cold and mountainous. We will be employed as a reconnaissance unit and will swan off into the mountains to do whatever mischief we can to the enemy, and keep the Yanks informed as to what we may encounter'.

The marines gave a little cheer. That seemed just about right!

'Any questions?' 'Duggie' asked. 'Sticky' Baines glared around with the intention of discouraging any inane remarks from the assembled troops. He succeeded; there was silence.

'Dismiss!' 'Sticky' saluted as the officers left.

We tumbled noisily from the mess hall, some back to their rooms, but the majority heading for the Seventh Cavalry beer hall. It was, 'She's a big fat bastard, twice the size of me' time! The beer flowed, the Beer Hall shook to the resounding tuneless roars of the marines. The married quarters of the Seventh Cavalry shook and vibrated for an entirely different reason, with a carefree vigour enhanced by the knowledge that the large cavalryman with the meat cleaver was no longer in camp!

CHAPTER TEN

To Join the Marines

'Embark!' The orderly lines of commandos disintegrated into somewhat of a noisy shambles as the various groups meandered to the waiting lorries. Again, all extraneous equipment had been put away in the stores and we were about to live on what we could carry on our backs. There was a little anxiety as, from the reports we had received, the war was all over bar the shouting. The lorries trundled through the Japanese countryside and we eventually arrived at the docks, to see a huge US navy transport waiting for us, rather than our old mate, the submarine *Perch*. At least we were not being conned this time!

After a sluggish but comfortable journey, we crawled sleepily on deck on the 16th November, to see, on the horizon, the dark low shape of the mainland of North Korea, with the low shabby buildings of the seaport of Hungnam. The transport gently stopped and the rattle of the anchor chain informed us that this was as far as we were to go. It was quite cold and we were glad of our protective clothing. As I belted on my equipment over the bulky parka, I sincerely hoped we wouldn't be expected to dash about with wild abandon whilst so dressed. I reckoned I would be severely knackered after about 50 yards!

There is a distinctive smell to the Orient which no photographs could possibly convey. The most attractive scenery loses some of its magic when it is accompanied by a spicy, slightly effluent aroma! Such was Hungnam. The first impression was that of a sea of mud engendered by the constant passage of marine heavy equipment. What may have been, in the past, attractive countryside, had been churned into an unmentionable morass by the heavy-tracked vehicles.

Crawling towards our transport were vehicles we would get to know as 'Amtraks' they were amphibious armoured vehicles; propelled by tank tracks and designed to carry troops ashore under inhospitable circumstances. The alarming design of these vehicles was that they lay very low in the water, and the amount of freeboard indicated that in rough conditions they would probably be quite easily swamped. Not so, however, on this occasion. The sea was like a millpond, and we clambered down the scrambled nets hanging from the side of the ship and into the Amtraks. The American crews of the strange vehicles were smiling and friendly as we crowded into the craft. In line ahead we plodded at a ridiculously slow rate towards the shore, the tracks of the craft churning up a heavy turbulence which changed to muddy brown as the tracks took a grip on the shallowing seabed. We trundled ashore and joined a vast convoy of transports of various types heading inland.

Eventually we rolled into a large tented town, row after row of American dung coloured bell tents. Everything in sight was stencilled with the large letters USMC. The US Marine Corps will go to tremendous lengths to ensure that they are 'Marines' they thus mark everything very clearly. We were to discover that they considered themselves the best and the greatest insult to offer them, was to indicate that they were members of the US Army . . . they hated the American Army and treated them with considerable disrespect. My knowledge, to date, had been gleaned from various old war films, where John Wayne, with his helmet at a jaunty angle and clearly marked U.S.M.C., knocked off Japs at an alarming rate and showed no fear . . . all of this to the invigorating sounds of heavy brass playing the marines song, *'From the Halls of Montezuma!'* To my amazement they were exactly as portrayed in the old war films. They had bravado to a degree which almost offended our natural British self-effacement. However, as time progressed we realised that, when the chips were down, they were not quite as good as they imagined themselves to be, but they weren't bad. It came as an awful shock to them, or at least the less experienced of them, to find that the Hollywood glamour of war didn't exist in reality and that the dead didn't just fall quietly down as in epics, but that bodies disintegrated into horrible obscene screaming pulp when struck by a missile. I am, however it reads, pro USMC. They were, without doubt, the best of the Yank armed forces; I considered that the average British Tommy was better, and that we were very much better soldiers!

We settled into our routine under canvas, learning to queue ankle deep in mud, with mess tins poised to receive dollops of food, which, even under these conditions, was surprisingly good. We were not yet cooking our own food from American 'C' rations, boxes of which were stored ready for issue when we eventually moved up country. It was whilst at the camp in Hungnam that we were joined by a motley crew of US Marine transport drivers who, with their trucks, had been seconded to the commandos. At last we had sufficient trucks to convey us wherever we wished to go. They were smashing blokes and appeared chuffed to have joined us. Among them was a Yank Marine who was posted to the Specialist troop, his name, Don Saunchegrow. He was a slightly built man, quietly spoken and modest, an attribute not shared by many of his countrymen. He had an ability to produce, apparently from out of thin air, wee luxuries, like booze and baccy at the drop of a hat.

So, for some days we kicked our heels impatient to be off before the bloody war ended. The only duty we performed was to take our turn watching the perimeter of Hungnam. Such had been the speed of the American advance that they were considerably stretched. There was a single track road heading north out of Hungnam to the hinterland where the enemy lay. This was the only road north and the mountainous terrain away from the road had seen little American presence, because the Yanks do like motorised transport and are reluctant to swan off out into the blue away from the sanctuary of their transport. This is a serious weakness and leaves the open spaces available for the enemy to hover threateningly!

Why bother anyway? The Gooks were beaten, the war was virtually over. This was the philosophy at the time. How wrong they were.

'Good News Percy' gathered us around him. He told us that at last we were off on the morrow. We would travel in our newly acquired transport some 60 miles inland. Our eventual destination was to be beyond the Chosin reservoir and towards the Manchurian border. Our first stop was to be at a small hamlet called Kotori. He informed us that there had been considerable rumour that Chinese troops had been spotted in the hills, but, he had been categorically informed by American intelligence that this was a load of cobblers!

CHAPTER ELEVEN

Bitten Off More 'n We Can Chew

The night of 27th November passed quickly as we slumbered comfortably in our heavily quilted sleeping bags. The warmth of the fireproofed quilt accentuated by the fierce heat of the carburetted petrol heaters, which threw out an unbelievable heat, coupled with an incredible extravagance in the amount of fuel used. This extravagance in the use of material by the Americans was a source of some amazement to our unit. They increased their logistical problems to almost insurmountable proportions by sheer gluttony in their equipment demands. However, we were warm, so what the hell.

As the morning arrived and we struggled from the tropical haze of our tents, we discovered that winter had arrived with a vengeance. The air was icy, the ground frozen. The contrast to our sauna-like tents was a physical blow. Now we were able to truly appreciate the luxury. I pitied those unfortunates under British command on the other side of the peninsular, they would have to manage in British winter gear . . . poor sods!

The line of waiting trucks had their engines roaring away. How on earth did they start the damn things? We noted that the canvas covers had been removed and that we would be open to the elements, unlike the other trucks waiting for the Yankee contingent, their covers were on. I was pleased to see this. Professionalism was being maintained. At least we would be able to retaliate quickly should some mishap befall the convoy. We mounted our trucks noisily and cheerfully. We were well fed, well equipped and raring to go. We would not, perhaps, have been so carefree had we known that, at about literally the same moment, hundreds and thousands of Chinese soldiers, whose country was not, even at this stage, involved in the war actively, were sweeping across the Manchurian border and melting into the mountains.

Even had we been aware of the impending clash, we would not really have been too deterred. Here we were, part of a magnificently equipped, huge international group of armies, armed to the teeth with the latest weaponry, backed by the world's wealthiest country, who could afford to transport to the war zone luxuries for the troops which were beyond the economic capabilities of most countries' populations in normal life. What were we faced with? A host of little yellow men existing on the minimum of rations, wearing skimpy quilted clothing, bearing antiquated weapons. We were on a collision course with an enemy we could piss all over without any bother at all! Ignorance was truly, on this occasion, bliss!

We huddled together, facing outwards in the open trucks. The engines roared and we headed up the narrow winding road. It was all up-hill. The higher we progressed into the mountains, the colder it became. I, like the others, could become completely self-contained at the drop of a hat. My warm sleeping bag, wrapped around my pack, enclosed two 24-hour 'c' ration packs, for emergency use. They contained, apart from contraceptives, all the necessities of life. Food, liquid, cigarettes, chocolate, matches and toilet paper. I smiled when I saw the toilet paper pack. I had four pairs of trousers of various shapes and design, starting with a pair of long johns. How in hell I was going to divest myself of these layers, to perform the natural function, I was buggered if I knew!

I looked round at my mates, they were all suffering the same emotions as myself. Our lips were already heavily chapped. The mucous in our nostrils frozen solid, with little icicles hanging from our nasal hair and our noses glowing like cigarette ends on a dark night. As we wended our noisy way, higher and higher along the road, which had become even narrower, the hard suspension of the vehicles coupled with the bumpy road caused us to be thrown from side to side in great discomfort.

As I sat facing outwards I gazed at the high mountains looking down on us and I felt slight unease as I peered at the threatening peaks.

Aware of the propensity of the Yanks to stick to the roads and their vehicles, I felt a little twinge of anxiety as to the possible current occupiers of those peaks. This tension was reduced slightly when we heard aircraft engines from the cruising American aircraft above us. I presumed that the Yanks had figured it was much easier to gaze down on the mountain-tops from the cockpit of an aircraft, rather than climb to the peaks. I thought to myself, this American instinct to always let the machine do the job, rather than put a man in jeopardy, could be the death of us all. I gripped my carbine just a little tighter . . . it was now my best friend and would be for some time to come.

I pondered Percy's words about US intelligence sources indicating that the presence of Chinese troops was not on, and I felt a little better. There can't, by now, be too many North Koreans left. The road now became even lumpier and I realised, with somewhat of a shock, that the lurching of the trucks was not only because of bad terrain, but also because of the presence of large numbers of shapeless lumps on the road. They, on perusal, became recognisable, but only just, as shapeless, mutilated and squashed bodies, the tattered uniforms revealing them to be North Koreans, very dead.

Ahead and to the right of us, as the convoy lumbered

relentlessly on, came the cackle of a machine gun. There is an eerie quality about gunfire when it is for real. The sound bears little relation to the same noises on a practice firing range or on the soundtrack of a film; the difference is indefinable, but it is there. We were some way towards the middle of the convoy of trucks and, therefore, not directly involved. The line of vehicles slowed momentarily. There was no indication of movement from the trucks. Had we been covered wagons in the old west, I feel sure we wouldn't even have formed a defensive circle such was the lack of concern shown.

Almost immediately, two aircraft wheeled towards a mountain peak ahead. Slowly and gracefully they passed across the mount in line ahead, and with an accelerating roar they zoomed skyward. They left behind them, poised in midair, two egg-shaped canisters, cartwheeling lazily towards the mountain from which the machine gun had been fired. They arched innocuously towards the offending occupants of the hill who had had the temerity to fire again, for, as the canisters struck the ground, a tremendous blast of fire and oily black smoke rolled forward, engulfing the entire mountain top area in a sea of hideous fire.

There were no cheers from the commandos, the silence seemed to express regret that men should die in such a manner . . . of course we wanted them to die before they had a chance to do us a mischief, but the manner of their dying seemed an obscenity beyond the expected overall obscenity which was war. It was terrifying to witness such power of destruction. The sadness changed to selfish instincts of self-survival as the thought crossed my mind, 'Thank Christ we have air supremacy and that won't happen to me.' The thought cheered me up and I promptly forgot the unfortunate orientals who had perished, at least until, a little later, we passed by the hill, the top of which was blackened, showing just the occasional flicker of fire. The black rolling smoke from the conflagration was billowing skyward carrying with it the souls of the poor bastards it had consumed.

The carbine in my hands seemed such a puny object, particularly as it was all I had to defend me against such horror. I again lowered the mental shield, for psychological survival, over my thoughts. Finally I put it behind me by, in a loud voice, calling to my mates with pseudo bravado, 'That'll teach them not to fart in Church!!'

There was muted laughter in the truck but it soon faded away as we trundled deeper into the Korean mountains and nearer the Manchurian border.

The road became steeper and narrower with every mile that passed, the trucks continued to rock and bump over the shapeless lumps that once had been men. The aircraft droned lazily overhead with the fire in their bellies poised to await the merciless call!

For hour after hour we snailed along the curving earth road. No sign of the enemy, for the North Koreans were now few and far between and the Chinese were biding their time before entering the conflict. This engendered a warm feeling of security and enabled us to concentrate on the extreme discomfort caused by the arctic weather conditions. The cold mountain winds were producing icicles around the furred hoods of our parkas as the warm, exhaled air surrendered to the superior power of the icy temperature. I had on two pairs of thick socks which were, in turn, encased in a pair of stout boots, yet my feet were bloody frozen! I wriggled my toes and remembered, longingly, the warm blazing fires of civvy street.

Some 40 miles on, as the crow flies, but considerably longer whilst traversing the winding road, we rounded the last bend. There before us lay what was once the small mountain town of Kotori. I noticed with pleasurable relief, small figures dotted on the crests of the hilltops overlooking the plain where the marine base existed.

At least we appeared to be in a properly protected encampment. Batteries of artillery were dug in here and there, not all of them pointing north towards Manchuria, but rather in all outward directions as though they were unaware exactly as to where their enemy lay. Tank crews loitered about their monsters of war, some washing clothes in their upturned helmets whilst others brewed coffee over fires. Row after row of USMC tents completed the picture.

There was an air of confidence about the place. The bustle was that of a victorious army, stopping briefly en route to the final knock out blow against an army now almost *hors de combat*. The marines and their equipment etched a warlike scenario in dark silhouette against the white snow.

As we disembarked from our vehicles, stiff and cold from the long journey, the Yanks evinced a casual interest which increased slightly when they realised that we were British. This mounted to complete camaraderie when they established that we were brother marines to boot!

The Royal Marine emblem incorporates a globe which has etched on it the European side of the world plus Asia. The US Marine Corps badge similarly displays the globe, but their globe maps the Americas and the Pacific. Quite soon after our arrival at Kotori I was comparing badges with a tall, unusually taciturn US marine. He looked at both emblems whilst chewing his gum, spat, paused, looked at me with a glint in his eye and said, 'Yup! You got one half, we got the other.' A long pause ensued as he continued to gaze at the badges. Finally he spoke. 'Yup! We both of us bitten off more'n we can fuckin' chew!'

With that he wandered off, still busily chewing gum, his helmet at a 'John Wayne' angle.

As always their hospitality was overwhelming in its

generosity. The main items proffered were five-pound tins of tea. They imagined, not without a grain of truth, that we were compulsive tea drinkers and we couldn't move for mountains of the stuff.

As we settled in to our temporary tented accommodation, brewing up frantically before the next batch of tea was offered, we became even more aware of the tremendous spirit of the Yank marines. They had just fought a series of successful battles and had bulldozed their way from South to North Korea. Another 100 miles and they would be astride the Manchurian border. Korea would have been liberated, or conquered, according to your point of view, and they would hopefully be able to shove off home. The icing on the cake was that the Supreme Commander, MacArthur, ego supreme, had promulgated an order of the day which indicated to the Yanks that expectations should include 'Home for Christmas!'

We meandered from our tents as we heard the roar of a large number of heavy aircraft passing low overhead. Looking skyward I saw a host of large twin-boomed transport planes slowly lumbering past. From the rear of the aircraft tumbled scores of packages which blossomed forth cascades of parachutes, which enabled the manna from heaven to land unbroken on the frozen ground. Among the packages were quantities of very special food, for, unbeknown to we British, today in America was Thanksgiving Day. Within hours, with the efficiency for which Americans are renowned, the Yankee cooks had produced, from some of the parcels recently airdropped from the fat-bellied transports, the most magnificent Thanksgiving dinner. The roast turkey steamed and shimmered beneath the blobs of cranberry sauce. Blueberry pie to follow and all the trimmings. Our mess tins groaned as the delicious food was crammed into every available space. All the food was fresh, no tinned rubbish for such an occasion. Though very enjoyable, it occurred to me that sometimes it was possible to mollycoddle. No wonder they were

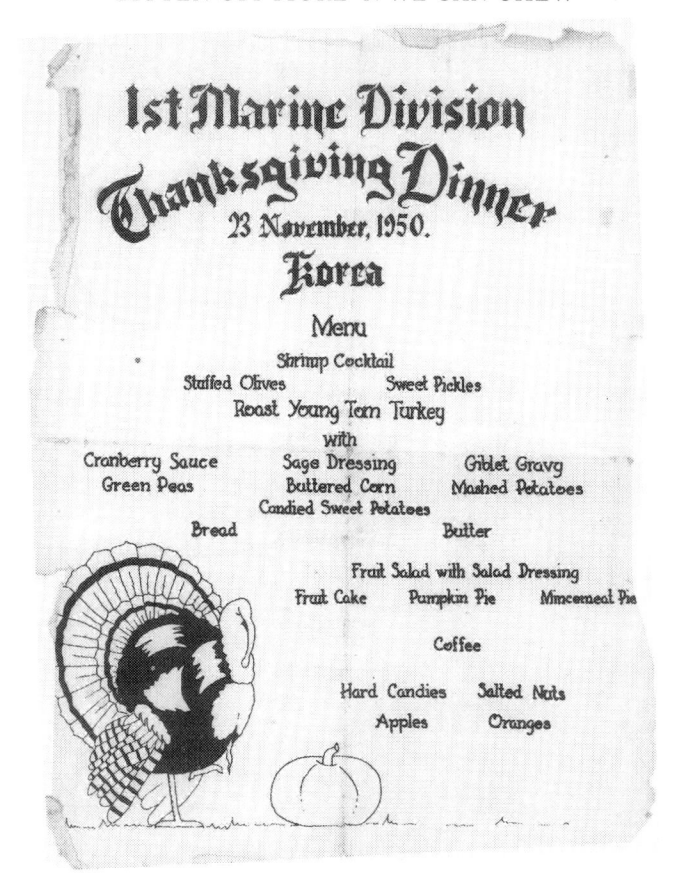

> **1st Marine Division**
> **Thanksgiving Dinner**
> 23 November, 1950.
> **Korea**
>
> Menu
>
> Shrimp Cocktail
> Stuffed Olives   Sweet Pickles
> Roast Young Tom Turkey
> with
> Cranberry Sauce   Sage Dressing   Giblet Gravy
> Green Peas   Buttered Corn   Mashed Potatoes
>   Candied Sweet Potatoes
> Bread   Butter
>
> Fruit Salad with Salad Dressing
> Fruit Cake   Pumpkin Pie   Mincemeat Pie
>
> Coffee
>
> Hard Candies   Salted Nuts
> Apples   Oranges

not too keen to take to the hills. With their distended bellies it was a wonder they had sufficient energy to climb aboard their transport, let alone gallop about in warlike posture. We sat about replete, belching after the magnificent repast, puffing manfully on huge cigars which were for 'afters'. A small entourage of American officers democratically passed among us. One of them, a huge man with much presence and radiating bonhomie, chatted to us affably. The stars on his uniform and the immediate response from his underlings indicated that he was of considerable status in the United States Marines. We were later informed, in hushed tones, that he was General 'Chesty' Puller, the bossman of this endeavour and much revered by the troops.

An indication of the severity of the weather was best illustrated when, after the meal it became necessary to perform the natural functions of waste disposal. Dotted round the camp were small, square, dilapidated tents. These contraptions disguised what were known in marine parlance as the heads. The heads were the lavatories. They consisted of deep pits bulldozed out of the solid frozen ground. At the edge of the pit were stretched two horizontal wooden struts. In configuration they resembled gymnasts' isometric bars, with the taller of the struts furthest from the latrine. One grasped the taller bar firmly and sat on the shorter one, with one's nether regions poised bare-arsed over the pit. Bearing in mind the extreme cold it was not policy to linger for too long. I mean, how embarrassing it would be shipped home with one's war wound being a frost-bitten penis!! The second and much more insidious danger was from the contents of the pit itself. As the effluence fell into the depths of the pit it immediately froze, and I do mean immediately! As a consequence the pits were rigid with pointed spears of excreta, frozen solid, upon which, if the unfortunate marine was careless enough to fall, he would impaled and suffer fairly unhygienic wounds. Humorous to contemplate but terrifying for the user as he clung with frozen hands to the strut and completed his ablutions with as much speed as possible.

One of the funniest sights in a not too hilarious situation was when a helicopter landed in the encampment too close to one of the heads. The whirling blades blew away one of the tents leaving, exposed to the elements, four marines, hanging on like grim death with their blue arses poised over the upturned swords of Damocles below, their expletives dissipating in the roaring currents of cold air from the helicopter!

CHAPTER TWELVE

Here Come The Chinamen

There seemed to be a certain amount of activity over and above the norm going on. The rumours began to circulate and once again I stripped and cleaned my carbine. If the bastard let me down I would never speak to it again! The unit officers had been in an enclave for some hours and at last we were gathered together for the customary chat as to intentions.

As we gathered in our groups the urgency of the situation was emphasised, as the American artillery started firing from their emplacements in the camp. What caused me a wee bit of consternation was the fact that they were firing in all directions, which indicated that the threat was not just from one direction. I pondered on the narrow road between us and Hungnam; it was our only way out if the shit hit the fan, which it obviously had.

Percy arrived. One day he would be the carrier of good news perhaps, but this was not to be the time.

'The Chinese have appeared in the hills in immense proportions.' This was his opening gambit. I felt a lump in the back of my throat. I swallowed it quickly because it was probably my arsehole! He continued his explanation. About 10 miles to the North was a town similar to Kotori, it was called Hagaruri. The 3rd Battalion of the Marine division had managed to withdraw from the hills under pressure from a number of Chinese regiments who had appeared from nowhere.

They were now trapped and surrounded in Hagaruri. Our job was to get through to them and then together, we would all withdraw back to Kotori. We would be accompanied by a company of US marines and a US army company, which would bring our total strength up to about 900 men. Between us and the Yanks we were to attempt to rescue, were an estimated three regiments of Chinese, and that was a conservative estimate! The one consolation, to us was that the rescue force was to be commanded by 'Duggie' Drysdale.

Captain Ovens looked around slowly as though contemplating the morale of his entourage. As my future was to be very firmly in his hands I returned the gaze and really looked at him for the first time. He was probably aware that we referred to him as 'Percy:' it was a nickname tinged with a lot of respect, as was our reference to Colonel Drysdale as 'Duggie', never ever, of course, to their faces. Percy was, as were we all, very scruffy at this moment. His large black moustache fairly bristled with the trauma of the moment. I searched anxiously at his very dark eyes to attempt to detect a glimmer of doubt as to our situation. They radiated confidence . . . I was not fooled for a moment . . . we were deeply in the shit!

As we wandered off to get ourselves kitted up for the fray, 'Sticky' Baines marched past, 'Good luck lads,' he winked, for one moment relaxing from his RSM stance. As his face creased into a gentle smile, he revealed that, beneath his tough exterior, he was a kind and gentle man as I was subsequently to discover.

The younger, relatively inexperienced marines in my section, who were soon to learn, quickly, skylarked together. Different in their backgrounds and attitudes. Polly Perkins, the brash cockney, full of beans, took the micky loudly out of Lew Heard, a brother Londoner, who took not the slightest notice. Reuben Nicholls and Reg Higgs, two extremely large and competent men, donned their equipment and chatted quietly to Ray Ogle, a dour Yorkshire man who was even larger in stature. Of the five only one was to survive the next 24 hours unscathed.

At last the unit was lined up and ready to go. Percy broke the good news. I was to take my lot, collect mine detector gear from the stores, and head north along the road to Hagaruri clearing the mines in the path of the relief forces.

We left the unit waiting for the off and headed towards the perimeter of the encampment, which also pointed us in the direction of the threatening hills on either side of the narrow road. We passed a company of Yank marines who were sitting on the side of the road. Then our first glimpse of the American army. They were also on the side of the road, waiting. Their apprehension was obvious. Their platoons consisted of mixed white and black soldiers, with the odd South Korean soldier dotted here and there. After the bravado and élan, the Yank Marines came into view. They were to be our escort. We took our position at the head and waited.

'What are we doing here? Why aren't we with our lot?'

'We'll be joining them later,' I replied hopefully. I wondered what the commandos were doing behind all the others instead of in front, their usual slot.

About 100 yards further on I could see an abandoned Yankee Tank, its track shed, with a number of bodies beside it. Poor sods. They had obviously abandoned their vehicle after it had hit a mine and had been mown down. I tapped the wallet hanging from my belt to reassure myself that the wire cutters, pliers and other tools I may require to deal with any mines, were safely in position and readily available.

From the hill overlooking the tank came sporadic bursts of small-arms fire. The occasional whine of bullets, not thankfully too accurate, passed among us. The Chinese were obviously ensconced on the peaks. The usual response from the Yanks was air and artillery attack and, as always, the planes swooped over and the artillery shells began to burst on the hill. After a quarter of an hour of projected carnage the Yanks ceased fire and we prepared to move off.

As we clambered to our feet, to our amazement we were greeted by yet another fusillade of fire from the hill. The Chinese, unlike their North Korean counterparts, had obviously abandoned the hill after opening fire, and returned after the long range attack looked as though it would be a long wait . . . but no!

'Look at them motherfuckers go!' A loud shout from the Yank marines accompanied us.

I looked up to the hill at which the Yank was pointing. There, in extended line, I could see, racing up the hill towards the Chinese, bayonets glistening, shouting fiercely, the commandos in full cry. This must have been a rare sight for the Yanks. As the green bereted marines disappeared over the crest I felt a tremendous surge of both pride and affection for my mates up there. A slight delay and then a flare arced into the sky. The Yanks cheered and off we went. I felt considerably comforted. The hills, where possible, would be attacked by the commandos as we progressed along the vulnerable road.

The system we used had to be modified somewhat because of the frozen state of the ground. Using a combination of the electronic mine detector and the antiquated but effective system of probing the ground, where possible, with metal probes, we inched our way towards Hangaruri many miles ahead. At every suspicious object a cone was placed nearby and my job was to investigate it and deal with it. A little way back our Yank marine escort watched and guarded us.

We were able to work uninterrupted for some time, and then, as I lay prone on the snow-covered ground, carefully easing away a layer of snow to reveal a wooden box, I became aware, with a start, that the splashes of snow occurring within feet of me and my mates, were being caused by small-arms fire from yet another hill. Discretion being, on this occasion, the better part of valour, I rolled away from the box mine and into a ditch on the side of the road and started to fire back at the puffs of smoke. Apart from the normal risk from gunfire, I had decided, temporarily, to abandon the box anti-tank mine, because, should one of the bullets hit the pressure plate on the top of the mine, it would definitely explode and I was not over-keen to partake in this one-sided silly game, for the moment.

I was not even sure whether my puny carbine was reaching the unfriendly Chinese on the hill, but it made me feel a little better to be doing something slightly aggressive rather than just lie there and think of England! My blokes had also taken up firing positions, as they were trained to do, and were responding to the unfriendly orientals.

'What you doin' boy?' I stopped what I was doing and looked up, in some amazement, at a Yank marine. He was standing on the road, in full view, firing inaccurately from the hip, at the looming hill. It was the John Wayne syndrome again. The helmet at the usual rakish angle, though no gum chewing on this occasion.

'Get down you fucking idiot,' I called.

Still firing, without aiming, in the general direction of the enemy, he gazed down at me, as I returned his stare with mounting incomprehension.

'Think about it, boy,' he drawled in a deep southern accent. ' The way you are, the only place they can git you is in the head!' The logic of this homespun philosophy astounded me. I even began, for one mad moment, to believe that he was possibly right, and that all of my training had been bull. He turned away from me and started to reload his rifle, or 'piece' as the Yanks called it.

I heard a fleshy smack, it sounded like a midwife's heavy hand colliding with the bottom of a new born babe. It was followed by a muted grunt as the Yank was thrown to the floor. He lay there for a few brief moments, twitching. The spurt of brilliantly coloured blood spread over the white snow. The bottom half of one leg was a tangled mass of flesh and shattered bone. No clean wound this!

Then he screamed, loudly, 'Medic, medic, medic!'

In a brief second, Reuben had dragged the injured marine into the safe haven of the ditch. He was white with shock and shivering as a medical orderly crawled towards him and began to dress his wound. Some moments later, with a large 'M' stencilled on his forehead to indicate that he had received an injection of morphine, a stretcher arrived to take the marine away. He was, by now, quite drowsy, but as he was carried away he called, 'I'm goin' home, I'm goin' home!'

He waved, smiled contentedly and was gone. The only indication of his presence was a rapidly freezing pool of red blood on the ground. In a way I envied him: he was indeed on his way home . . . at least he wouldn't die. I had just witnessed a perfect example of a self-inflicted wound administered by the enemy!

The US Marine Air Corps interrupted the proceedings by incinerating the hilltop. In the quiet few moments before the flames died down, we nipped over to the offending box mine, attached a hook and line to it, and after carefully examining the ditch in which we lay, for possible booby traps, pulled the bloody thing clear. Quite often, in mine warfare, the enemy are aware that mines are pulled from the ground if there is a suspicion that it is booby trapped. Therefore, they will booby trap a nearby piece of cover where it is likely that the engineer will take cover whilst doing so. On this occasion neither the mine or the ditch was booby trapped, so all was well.

After a further hundred yards or so of probing, listening to the electronic device and searching without result, occasionally crawling to cover as an inhospitable Chinaman endeavoured to disturb our concentration by shooting us, the powers that be decided that we had passed through the minefield and all was now safe. With a cackle of metallic orders from our radio we packed our gear and squatted in the ditch as the convoy started past us.

After about a dozen trucks had roared past I heard the familiar tones of Don our American Marine driver. 'Hop aboard, fellahs. Hagaruri here we come!'

We clambered over the tailboard and as we sat, facing outwards, I lit a cigarette and was surprised to note that my hands were shaking a little. The psychological stress of dealing with items which were capable of, and even designed to, remove bits of one's body if one makes a mistake, is difficult to measure, but have no doubt, it does disturb one's equilibrium for a little while!

Suddenly the trucks jerked to a halt, and as they did so there was some fairly intensive firing from the hills alongside. I tumbled over the side of the truck. I was not alone. In our hurry we left our heavy packs, sleeping bags and rations in the truck. I was not too worried about this because when the fracas was over I was sure that we would return to the lorry and restart our journey.

As we left the road authoritative voices called, 'Get off the road and up the hill'

We struggled up the hill, a mixture of British and Americans. We started slowly and our speed increased with the intensity of the gunfire which was coming from the opposite hill on the other side of the road. Fortunately it seemed all to be rifle fire, nothing of heavier calibre.

At that moment two incidents occurred, both of which browned me off considerably. The first was a bright flash and gentle boom as the truck containing all our gear disintegrated. Any hope I may have had of rescuing any of the equipment disappeared as the remnants of the truck burst into flames. What a bastard; the 'C' Rations I had carefully shepherded for miles were now cooking merrily away. My beautiful, warm, cosy sleeping bag was no longer fire proof. Like any old hobo I was the proud possessor of that which I was wearing, and nothing else.

The second of the two incidents not only disturbed me, but also caused a traumatic cessation of my heartbeat, because, as I turned from the sad sight of my equipment going up in smoke, I realised that the shooting from the far side of the truck had ceased. I soon realised why, when I heard a bugle call and a blast of whistles. Bugle call? What pratt was blowing on a bugle at such a time? As dark figures appeared over the crest of the hill above me and my mates, I realised that the bugler was of oriental ancestry and the call was urging his compatriots to charge down the hill to do us a mischief. It was going to be one of those days!!

North Korean mountain landscape is similar in terrain to the wilds of northern Scotland, with the added delight that it is considerably more arctic in temperature. From the soldier's point of view it is a dead loss. There is little vegetation to hide behind and the ground is too frozen to dig into. The inability to be able to hide is a considerable embarrassment when one is deeply in the mire. The disadvantages in my current situation were accentuated by the aggressive intent of the quilted figures appearing over the crest of the hill. There seemed to be an awful lot of them and they were walking, not running. Their features were indistinct but their intentions were crystal clear. Though they were still some 500 yards away I wondered what the occasional bright flash was, until, in a heart-stopping moment I realised that it was the reflection from their bayonets which were affixed to their rifles. There is a well-known comic saying in British military circles that certain races, particularly

Germans, 'Don't like it up 'em', indicating that the mere sight of cold steel will cause them considerable fright. At this moment I became aware that the paraphrase also applied to me. The last thing I wanted was oriental cold steel probing my anatomy. The flippant description I have made of the situation in no way indicates the sheer terror I felt.

In the Second World War a British officer was asked to describe his emotions during the battles at Dunkirk. With typical British phlegm he said, 'Oh dear, the noise, the people.'

The noise in the current situation, was loud and confused, with the crackle of small-arms fire enhanced by the boom and crash of artillery. The singing 'ping' of small-arms fire and the babble of voices as far apart, in accent, as Manchester and New York, all added to the cacophony that was rapidly becoming a night-mare. I rolled on to my side and drew my bayonet and, with trembling fingers, after many attempts attached it to my stupidly small carbine. Alongside me, very still, was a Yankee soldier. His face was cradled in his hands, his rifle, with bayonet fixed, was beside him, untouched. I was transfixed with a terrible anger; he should be helping, not just lying there.

I reached out and punched him on the shoulder. 'Come on you bastard . . . don't just lay there, do something!'

I pushed him and he rolled onto his side, face towards mine, or rather, what was left of his face. The bullet had struck him in the region of the nose, the entry had disintegrated his face and his eyes protruded on long yellow stalks. My sympathy for him lasted about a second, because the emotion was overwhelmed by a tremendous surge of delight at my good fortune. Standards of decency are rapidly lost in a self-survival situation.

I greedily reached for his rifle, a much more effective weapon than my carbine. I drew my knife and cut his ammunition bandoliers, which were of canvas manufacture, and dragged them towards me. But not completely, for the memory of that moment of callousness returns to me, with some regret, at every Remembrance ceremony I have attended in the years since then.

The pleasure of the fierce thump on my shoulder as I fired the rifle made my spirits surge. Alongside me soldiers and marines were settling down to what was to become a turkey shoot. The elation began to subside a little with the realisation that, though lots of the Chinese were falling over and lying still, there always appeared to be another to take his place, and they were inexorably drawing closer. They didn't seem to be wearing helmets, but little quilted caps and I noted, with a start, that some of them did mot appear to be carrying weapons. I could picture a little Chinaman pushing me to one side, as I had the Yank, and nicking my newly purloined rifle. The thought spurred me into a furious rate of fire.

A tremendous roar filled my ears, a crescendo of noise which lasted but a split second, and then silence. The world stood still as the flight of American aircraft crossed our bows, following their brothers who had taken us by surprise. The air was filled with spiralling egg-shaped containers, which with deceptively slow acceleration, were descending on the lines of Chinese soldiers about 200 yards away. They broke in disorder and started back in the direction from which they had come. I watched in fascination as their demise drew closer. We had stopped firing and could hear the distressed cries of the poor bastards as they ran. Some of them dropped to the ground and curled up into the embryo position, they had given up and were already dead!

The elation within me ceased in a millisecond as I rolled onto my back and anxiously searched the skies above me for spiralling containers. I sighed with relief; the air above us was clear. Some of the Yank Air Force have previous convictions for mistakenly napalming their own troops . . . but not this time, thank Christ!

With a thundering roar the hill in front of us became Hades.

I burrowed my head into my arms, partly to protect me from the tremendous surge of heat blasting towards us, and partly to shelter my susceptibilities from the terrible screams of men burning to death. The screams did not last long. The ultimate horror as two men, screaming and engulfed in flames, ran towards us. Their movement causing the flames to intensify as their bodies were being consumed. In an attempt to shorten the ghastly proceedings as soon as possible I fired at the poor demented sods. I was not alone, the rattle of rapid fire from our side quickly ended their agony. But not ours, as the stench crept towards us in the smoke. I felt the bile rise in my stomach. But in the state of mind induced by the intervention of fire which had saved our bacon, I prayed to myself, and even thanked God for the invention of napalm. The instinct of survival rapidly removes the thin veneer of civilisation, of that there is no doubt.

It was unfortunately necessary to follow up the napalm attack and move to the crest of the hill, so recently the scene of such carnage. I reluctantly clambered to my feet. I removed the mechanism from my discarded carbine and threw it as far as I could, and headed up the hill. As I started off up the hill I looked around me and saw to my dismay, that the convoy was moving off along the road, still heading towards Hagaruri, and that it appeared that maybe we were being left behind. The majority of the troops in our ensemble were Yankee soldiers with just a smattering of one or two green berets intermingled in no particular order. It was apparent that the convoy was under attack which was being broken up because of the air superiority we were enjoying. God help us when nightfall came and we lost that edge!

'Back to the road. Move, move!' The authoritative American accent was immediately responded to, as we had just arrived at the point where the charred, twisted bodies, still smoking indicated the horror of the recent napalm attack. As we stumbled down the hill in disorganised haste the small group of green berets gravitated towards one another. I could see no other commandos at all in the group and realised that we were now at the back end of the convoy and, what was the cause of some anxiety, we were with an Army company. Such was the antipathy between the Yank marines and their army compatriots, that a little of the marine propaganda had taken a firm grip within my mind; therefore, unfairly or not, I had little confidence in them. Still, one consolation, I was with four or five of my own blokes: they at least could be relied upon. As we arrived back onto the narrow earth road, the battered trucks were already on the move. The wagon train was rolling. A slight disadvantage was that our wagon, with others, had been destroyed, with all of our kit. The tribal instinct had taken control and I had an overwhelming urge to find the commandos and rejoin them as soon as possible. I was fairly well pissed off! No unit, no rations, no sleeping bag to survive the intensely cold night ahead, and to round it off we appeared to be with an offshoot of the main convoy and some distance behind it. Not one of my better days.

CHAPTER THIRTEEN

Alone, All Alone

We had managed to clamber aboard an open truck containing about 12 Yanks. Their morale was evidently fairly low. A few, with spirit, faced outwards in the truck clutching their weapons and ready for any trouble, of which there was no shortage! The remainder huddled on the floor of the truck ... I felt they would pack it all up without the slightest hesitation should the situation seriously deteriorate.

In the corners of the truck, unattended and awaiting our attention, sat two Yankee 24-hour ration packs. The boxes were almost calling out to be plundered, and they were. My share was two unidentified tins, no pretty labels on these, and three cigarettes which I hastily stuffed into my parka pocket. I felt considerably cheered by my good fortune. This satisfaction with my fate began to deteriorate a little when I realised that the light was beginning to fade. I looked at the lads and touched the top of my head with the palm of my hand. This was marine parlance for, close in on me, which they immediately did. Lew Heard was dwarfed by the large confident stature of Reuben Nicholls. I looked anxiously to see if the cheerful Polly Perkins was amongst us, he was not. I hoped he was all right. The other two marines I knew by sight, but their names escaped me for the moment. They were all quite young and at 26 years of age I felt like a grandfather!

'Look lads, we have got to stick together. We can't rely on these fuckers.' I waved my arm towards the sorry-looking soldiers, and continued, 'After dark we will probably have to abandon the truck. We mustn't be separated, okay?'

They nodded agreement and we each retreated physically to our previous outward-facing positions and mentally withdrew and pondered on our individual dilemmas.

I peered anxiously into the deepening gloom. The silhouette of the hill peaks began to lose their sharp intensity, and as the shadows deepened I felt the temperature begin to fall at an alarming rate. The trucks rumbled jerkily on at a slow pace.

'Our father, which art in heaven, hallowed be thy name. . .'

It was me, I came to with a start. I was bloody praying quietly to myself.

'Come on, Brady . . . pull yourself together. He won't help you.'

My thoughts raced. One thing I determined, whatever happened, I was not going to surrender. Sod that for a game of soldiers!

The deepening gloom became night. The Yankee pilots would be back at base now, quaffing a well-earned double whisky. The skies overhead were clear now, sad news for us, but a source, I am sure, of considerable pleasure for the Chinese. In news bulletins the Chinese were always referred to as 'hordes'. I wondered how many Chinese required to be termed a horde? At Army Group level I suppose it would have to number thousands. At my level, at this precise moment, feeling as I did, two would be a horde!

The bright winter moonlight was also bad news. Heavy cloud would have been perfect. I remembered the brimming mess tins a short few hours before. I would have settled for some Thanksgiving turkey at that moment. I could almost smell the steaming food then my reverie was disturbed in a flash. The occupants of the truck visibly stiffened as the plaintiff tones of a bugle wafted towards us from the dark hills. The situation was so stupid, I was overwhelmed with anger. A little line of trucks, separated apparently from the main body, with no scouts out at all to monitor the outer limits of the road. It was ridiculous! If they would just stop the trucks and let us dig in to a defensive position for the night, until those lovely aeroplanes with their lovely, lovely, napalm could arrive, at daylight, and burn up all the nasty Chinamen. Surely, God, that wasn't too much to ask?

'Boom!' As a crimson flash lit up the convoy, flames could be seen flickering from a truck ahead. Everything stopped. We sat uneasily in the stationary vehicle. Everywhere was complete, frightening silence. Then with an ear-piercing blast, whistles came from the darkness at the side of the road. As we rolled over the side and onto the frozen road, volleys of small-arms fire struck the trucks. Complete pandemonium ensued. Shouts and screams intermingled with the rattle of fire, the occasional sharp crack of a hand grenade as I wriggled in an attempt to get off the road and into the scrub vegetation alongside. The bulky clothing was an encumbrance beyond measure and I toyed with discarding my parka, but common sense prevailed. I had not yet fired my rifle and could see no point in blasting away at nothing. In spite of all my plans for mutual action, all the training for concerted activity goes for a burton under such circumstances. We of the Commando had a tremendous advantage over the Yanks. Our training was mainly designed to produce the ability to fight at night, whilst they, poor buggers, were blazing away wildly. To fire wildly at night produces muzzle flash on which the enemy can register. This was happening and Yanks were dying. Hollywood interpretations of war had been transplanted and Dante's Inferno had become the reality.

It was fairly obvious to me that it would be a good idea to get off the road and away as soon as possible. The pad of footsteps passed across my front and I fired two shots at the fleeting shadows. The reply was a burst of fire of such intensity that I am sure I burrowed some inches into the frozen ground as the whine of bullets passed me. From that moment on I had left any resemblance of civilisation and become a berserk inhabitant of an abattoir. I was surrounded in the dark by leaping, shouting shadows, the screams of wounded and dying men echoing through the night. After shooting several enemy at close range, I decided to fix my bayonet to my rifle in case I ran out of ammunition, but to my abject horror it would not go on. I suddenly realised that I had a carbine bayonet and the correct bayonet for the larger Garand I now carried was in the scabbard, on the body of the faceless Yank. I felt punished for the theft of his rifle by the incompatibility of my bayonet.

Out of the darkness, I saw running shadows heading towards me and in the sporadic light of fires and bursting grenades, I saw they were a line of quilt-jacketed Chinese. As one stumbled into me, I shouted, and bayonet in hand, I lashed out at the dark shape, stabbing him in the face. His shriek of pain was cut short, he fell and whatever part of his head had been pierced, refused to release my blade and he and my bayonet fell to the dark ground and joined the other bodies lying there.

I remember being trained not to fire rapidly or indiscriminately because I would run out of ammunition. The enemy did not co-operate and a close-range melee ensued, me shooting at anything that moved. Whichever of my mates that might have been nearby just did not exist. I was fighting for my very survival, amazed that none of the noisy bullets hit me; it was a miracle. Suddenly there was silence. I appeared to be the only one in the close vicinity to be completely unharmed. I could hear the shouts of the next wave of the enemy scrunching through the snow to finish off the survivors. 'Time to fuck off out of here!' I thought, as I buried myself against the in-coming bullets.

A figure beside me shouted, 'I'm hit, God help me . . . help me . . . medic, medic!'

The accent was American, for a moment I hesitated. Heroes dash into situations careless as to their own fate. I pondered whether to get off the road or go to the assistance of the Yank. Self-preservation won as a further fusillade of shots indicated that prudence was the only choice. Selfishly and shamefully I continued to crawl away from the road. In self-analysis I justified my movement away from the Yank by pretending that I was, at least, crawling towards the enemy. It was bullshit. I was frightened and had the tremendous urge to survive, come what may. That my actions may have been different had the accent been British is further proof that the tribal instinct lurks within all of us. The Yank was now silent and probably dead. I felt my pockets as I thought of the wounded Yank and felt a surge of relief when the small pack of morphine syringes came to light, not out of sympathy for him but rather preparation for my comfort should the same fate befall me. Selfish bastard! But still alive!

I was now some yards from the road and I peered through the moonlight hoping to see one or two of the commandos; nothing. Around me, quiet and still, were a number of human forms. Whether dead or alive I didn't know. I stayed as still as they were, as I heard padding footsteps move towards me. With a surge of adrenalin, I realised that the silent figures were Chinese soldiers, armed and aggressive, moving towards the convoy some 20 yards away.

'Surrender, surrender. Every man for himself.' The plaintive voice registered absolute defeat. It was the voice of a man who had made a decision which was quite right under the circumstances. It was a decision I was not going to consider at this time, not out of bravado, but merely that my chances of survival, though apparently slim, were infinitely better as a temporary free agent rather than as a guest of the Chinese.

The silent figures passed on either side of me and the other recumbent figures. When they had progressed beyond me and towards the trucks, I started to slowly crawl away. In the moonlight I could see figures near the trucks clambering to their feet with arms held high. I looked for the shapes of berets, but could see only helmets. I wondered how my blokes were. The firing was dying away as more surrendered. The night became quieter as I slowly increased the distance between myself and the aggressive enemy. Many yards further on it was necessary to lie still again as a posse of Chinese passed nearby. Their victory was apparent because they were no longer silent but chatting softly in the quaint singsong sound of their language. My morale was fairly low at this stage, because I had decided to head south towards the haven of Kotori from which we had embarked some hours before. My problem was that I was completely disorientated and hadn't got a bloody clue which way was south!! I would have to wait till daylight. I could not hide up during darkness because I was too bloody cold and only by constant movement could I be sure of survival overnight.

At last I stood up and made progress, hopefully south, though with my luck I was probably heading towards Peking! I relaxed just a little and plodded through the snow.

'I've made it. Thank you God!' I mumbled to myself.

Had I had enough time I would have definitely defecated when, to my abject horror, some yards ahead of me a figure rose out of the snow. As I threw myself down into the deep snow, I had a vague impression of an oriental face displaying as much fright as I myself was feeling. The Chinaman's face was partly shadowed by the soft peak of a quilted hat. His looping arm released a dark object which swooped towards me as I buried myself in the snow.

'A grenade, a grenade. Christ help me!' My brain sparked the message of fear to every nerve fibre in my body. I crunched deeper inundated in terror. I counted . . . 'One, two, three, four.' No explosion. I was aware that grenades carried by infantrymen usually have fuses which delay for either four or seven seconds. All was silent, the only explanation was that the device had misfired. I couldn't believe that yet again I was in luck, though, of course, luck is relative to one's situation. I had instinctively rolled to my right as I fell so that I was where I had last been seen by the oriental. I twisted myself into a firing position hardly daring to breathe, and cautiously and slowly raised my head. Somewhere, within 35 feet of me was an unfriendly soldier, as frightened as I, who had just missed his first chance. I had to be sure he didn't have a second. I listened. The concentration one can give at times like this will never ever be equalled in such intensity again in your life. So, I listened for my Chinese friend. I could hear, away in the distance, the tap, tap, tap of small-arms fire. I looked; short-lived surges of light silhouetted the skyline and preceded the onerous booms of explosions. But close at hand . . . nothing! 'Where are you, you bastard?' My eyes vainly attempted to pierce the gloom for a sight of my foe, but no luck! All was shaded white and still.

The wet sound of feet on snow caused me to raise my head in fear. My eyes were like organ stops as they focused on the Chinaman as he scrambled to his feet. To my immense relief I saw that he was slipping and sliding in his haste as he ran. A further heartening discovery was that his hands, which he was waving about to assist his balance on the treacherous surface, were empty . . . no gun! At first sight he appeared to be unarmed. I was following his movement with the foresight of my rifle. To my surprise he fell heavily to the snow. I was even more surprised to note that a faint whisp of smoke issued from the barrel of my rifle, I had, without even realising it, shot the bastard. Serves him bloody right! 'You bloody fool.' I was talking to myself again. The noise of my gun would surely alert any of his mates who happened to be nearby. I felt like a lover who had sneezed whilst hiding in the wardrobe after the unexpected arrival home of the husband.

Lack of control had made discovery almost inevitable. 'Must get away from here.' I really thought that I must do something about the habit I had developed, that of talking to myself. The pressure of events was definitely driving me round the bend.

As I slogged past my erstwhile opponent I glanced guiltily down at him. He was spread-eagled, face down and motionless, apparently very dead. I did not linger but had it away on my toes . . . not too quickly though. One could rapidly become a fatality in this tremendously cold temperature if one sweated copiously and then rested and allowed it to freeze against the body later. As I trudged on I was still hoping fervently that my direction was south.

The inhospitable terrain was so bleak that, as the first flush of the dawn light slowly pushed aside the night's darkness, and I became fully aware of my situation, I became so pissed off that I seriously contemplated the possibility of throwing my hand in, should much more go wrong. The usual interminable Korean hill, on the side of which I clumsily made my way, would be replaced by another and then another as I progressed. There were a number of tasks which had to be accomplished fairly soon before daylight. It was time to search for somewhere to hide up during the daylight hours. I was overwhelmed by loneliness and badly needed companionship and advice. The first priority, however, was food and a cigarette, in that order. The cigarette would have to wait till darkness had gone but I contemplated, with relish, consuming the contents of one of my purloined ration tins. As the weak wintry sun peeped over the hill crests I was able, at last, to sort out my direction of travel. The sun appeared slightly to my right and behind me. At a rough guess this indicated that I had been travelling slightly south-west . . . ah well . . . better than due north! *If* I hadn't been travelling in circles during the long night I would need to change course to the south-east, to bring me back on to a rough heading towards Kotori . . . my haven! I had also to take into account that I was very cold and exceptionally exhausted. All in all, to coin a phrase, I was deeply in tripe!

    I settled into a dip in the ground, which supplied a little shelter from the wind and partially hid me from view. I took the smaller of the two tins from my pocket and decided that now was the time to have a wee snack. God, the weather was so bad. My lips were chapped and raw and icicles clogging the fur of my parka hood were almost permanent features by now. I needed the sustenance of food to provide body heat. I was dull with tiredness and all in all in quite a sorry state. I could not remove my mittens because of the deep cold and held the tin clumsily whilst I used my knife to prise off the lid. As the contents appeared, my dismay was absolute. There, in all its nutritious glory, was an icy concoction of fruit cocktail!! Little cold chips of pineapple, pear and orange. I was certain that when I had completed my meal I would be colder than before! I rapidly consumed the contents: anything was better than nothing!

CHAPTER FOURTEEN

Thank God For Percy

Daylight slowly engulfed me with its slightly higher temperature which was a little more comfort. I just had to sleep. I thought longingly of my warm sleeping bag, now a heap of ashes in a burnt-out truck. I remembered the warmth of childhood and the delight of a cosy bed and being tucked in tightly by a devoted mother. My thoughts raced through all the warm memories of comfort I had enjoyed in the past, as I settled myself in the foetal position. My eyelids dipped and a pleasurable lethargy overwhelmed me. I was aware that what I was doing was stupid, that I should keep going. All the lessons taught about survival in cold climates emphasised that to lie down and give in was probably an invitation to self destruction . . . I didn't bloody well care any more. Sod it, I was going to have a kip if it killed me, and it probably would! As my mind relaxed, various visions wandered incoherently through my befuddled brain. I thought of the American pilots, refreshed and eager after a good night's sleep, clambering into the cockpits of their vicious war machines which carried, like mother hens, eggs in their bellies, only their eggs were brimful of napalm. I opened one eye as the realisation struck me that from the air there would be little to distinguish me from a Chinese soldier, particularly as I was in what was now Chinese-controlled territory. The horror and fear contained deep inside me, of the napalm flames, woke me immediately. I would have to camouflage myself very carefully indeed before I did lapse into unconsciousness. I struggled tiredly to my feet, glanced around, and immediately dropped back into my small depression, both in the ground and in my mind! There, on the crest of the hill were a group of men. I should have expected the area to be fairly heavily inhabited by the Chinese army, and it apparently was!

'That's it!' I thought. 'Bollocks . . . I've had enough now.' I cautiously raised my head and looked for the men. A glimpse of green headgear made my heart jump. I had to watch my imagination in my condition. To me, green berets have the same effect as an oasis in the desert would have on a thirsty wanderer, and either could be mirages caused by wishful thinking. I shook my head to steady my thoughts and looked again. I leapt to my feet, shouted, and staggered towards them. They stopped, the lead figure turned towards me, smiled and waved me towards them. He was his usual calm unflurried self, radiating confidence, though maintaining the usual social difference between himself and the peons. It was Captain Ovens . . . Percy! I was chuffed and almost hysterically happy. I knew that all would be well now because I had such confidence in the man. My tiredness flew straight out of the window, the adrenaline flowed and all was well with the world!

His motley half-dozen consisted of himself and another commando and an assorted group of Yankee marines, one of whom was limping badly from a leg injury. In conversation I made the startling discovery that the road I had abandoned some long hours ago, was just over the hill about half a mile away. We were heading for Kotori on a course parallel to it!

The joy of being in friendly company coupled with the knowledge that Percy, in whom, I had supreme confidence, would get us all safely to our destination, produced a euphoria that normally would require a bellyful of beer to accomplish. He had obviously decided to travel through the daylight hours, with proper precaution being maintained. Like a wartime convoy we had to travel at the speed of the slowest ship, our slowest vessel was the Yankee marine with the severe limp. The routine had apparently been that each man took it in turn to help the marine. In spite of his incapacity he was tremendously cheerful and confident and did me the world of good.

The staccato clucking of the helicopter blades tuck-tuck-tucked overhead. We were about 100 yards from the valley heading towards Kotori, and the road, now empty, the scene of our disastrous defeat earlier. An American helicopter appeared over the crest, we waved like mad, partly to attract his attention and partly to indicate to him that we were not Chinese. I was aware that the machine could carry very few and pretended that my main anxieties were for the injured marine. Though, of course, had there been room for a few more, and had I been amongst the lucky few I would not be too distressed! The 'copter hovered some hundreds of feet in the air as the crew perused us to reassure themselves that it was not all a trap, set by the cunning orientals. Apparently satisfied, they commenced their descent towards us. When they were about 100 feet above us, the sound of a machine gun echoed through the valley. As the bullets whined around, the crew of the chopper bottled out and with a regretful wave, soared skywards. My joy changed rapidly to chagrin. I called them everything I could lay my tongue to. Later, in retrospect, I appreciate that they could not risk this machine for one injured man, but at the time I was furious! Not so Percy. With a shrug of the shoulders he carried on. The strange factor in all this, was that the Chinese were obviously laying up for the night hours because of their fear of the American Air Force, this allowed us to wander through unhindered. So we plodded on. With the exception of the limping Yank marine, we all looked a pretty sorry sight, but in reasonable condition. The poor Yank was quietly suffering, but no word of complaint passed his lips. I felt tremendously elated to be with them. Being deeply in the mire on one's own is fairly traumatic, but if others are also sharing the difficulties then one doesn't feel quite so victimised and alone. Information elicited from conversation conducted in exhausted grunts indicated that the relief force had been split by attacks from the flanks when night fell. Only the leading half of the convoy had got through to the Yanks at Hagaruri. The casualties had been disastrously high and, at this stage, we appeared to be among the only survivors.

This news shattered me. I retired into myself and pondered sadly on the possible fate of all my mates. Where were they now? How many had died in the battle? What would exaggerate the casualties and make survival the more difficult would be the extreme weather conditions. A simple wound would so easily become fatal with the combination of the extreme cold and unsophisticated Chinese Army medical care. I presumed that the Chinese medical services would be primitive in the extreme.

We were involved in a very eerie situation. There was no doubt that there were hundreds of Chinese all about us, cleverly camouflaged. We presumed that the helicopter would have reported our presence and that the cruising American aircraft were aware of our location and route. This comforting fact did not, however, still the stomach-churning unease as the aircraft passed overhead. They were like mother hens shepherding their chicks to safety. The presumption was that we were not being harried by the enemy because they did not want to betray their presence to the marauding aircraft and therefore invite the attention of napalm and rockets. Thank God I was not alone, as before. Communal fear is so much easier to give up the ghost! I was cheered by the sense of purpose and direction shown by

Percy, to whom I willingly abdicated all responsibility for my well-being. All I had to do was to keep plodding on, deep in thought, completely exhausted, through the snow. I was singularly grateful to have survived thus far, but was aware that there was still a long way to go!

Now it was my turn to help the injured Yank. Psychologically I saw it as penance for my conscience over the Yank who had called for help and been ignored by me, in my scramble for survival. I therefore approached the task with some enthusiasm in spite of my tiredness. He was obviously in considerable discomfort, but he was not short of bottle and not a word of complaint passed his lips, as he was helped along. The only sign of pain was the occasional grunt as we struggled on. After my stint another of the party undertook the task of assisting the Yank. The adrenaline producing elation of meeting survivors began to dissipate and exhaustion crept over me in waves. My head was slumped and I watched my feet sink into the deep snow as pace after pace forward took me closer to safety. I was not alone, the physical and mental anguish was clearly displayed on the faces of us all. I have seen photographs of men taken shortly after battle, where the gaunt and harrowed expressions, the fullness of the eye, indicate that survival has taken its toll of their nervous system. It is the common denominator which front-line soldiers display to differentiate between them and the calm, plump, well-fed appearance of non-combatant troops!

'We'll stop for 10 minutes.' Percy spoke softly.

We fell gratefully to the ground. Percy wandered across. Like us, he looked exhausted. His normal smart, dapper appearance had gone. Above his heavily iced moustache his eyes, though bloodshot, retained the intensity of purpose which indicated to me that all would be well!

'I'm glad you made it. What happened to your section?'

'Christ knows, Sir. We were separated when the shit hit the

fan. How far are we from Kotori?' My question betrayed the anxiety I was feeling.

'Not far now.' The tone of his voice was so reassuring that it was as effective as a comforting pat on the head. He passed to the others and had a quiet word with each. When he was satisfied that all was well he sat down himself, slightly apart from us and deep in his own thoughts.

I shook my water bottle . . . solid! The contents iced up. It takes an awful lot of snow to quench the thirst but at least it can be done, so that was one problem less. My mind wandered to my sole surviving tin of rations. I decided to hang on to it until I was desperate for food and also for the occasion when there may be less people about eager to share it!

The 10 minutes rest seemed to last about 10 seconds and we were, reluctantly, called to our feet again. The only sounds to be heard were the crunch of boot on snow, heavy breathing and the drone of cruising aircraft. The light seemed to be slightly dimmer than before, I remembered, with a start, my thoughts the night before as darkness descended . . . the same applied for the coming night, only more so! Christ help us when daylight completely faded and the little Chinamen crept from their wee foxholes, sheltered from the merciless aircraft by the welcome of darkness.

Mile after mile we progressed very slowly with a short rest every hour. The light began to fade

'God ... get me out of here. Let me survive and I'll never complain again, I'll even go to church!' I whispered assorted prayers to myself, my life as an agnostic being rapidly reassessed under the influence of fear. Alas, my sojourns with Christianity always faded rapidly when safe, only to reappear with enthusiastic brevity at the next time of stress. I am, currently, an agnostic and will probably remain so until the final moments come, when I will temporarily embrace Christ, not out of love or belief, but just in case those holy ones amongst us were right and I was wrong! I believe that this is referred to as the sin of presumption . . . that'll do me nicely. I am the supreme presumptive – enjoy the vices and back it both ways, just in case! As Punch said to Judy, in a high-pitched voice, 'That's the way to do it!'

As darkness descended we did not stop. My morale dropped alarmingly. Every sound, every bush, became a Chinaman. I concentrated on the back of the man in front of me as we continued our lethargic way in single file. We stopped suddenly, by colliding into one another like a goods train coming to a halt. The metallic click of rifle mechanism could clearly be heard ahead. There followed a whispered conversation. One of the voices was American and the other Percy's cultured tones. Off we stumbled again and I started, alarmed, as a number of holes in the ground appeared in the gloom. The shapes in the holes revealed themselves as American Marines. 'Thank you, God, thank you, God!' I grunted in the elation of the moment. It was almost an anticlimax when I realised that we were passing through the outer line of defences of Kotori, we were home! A wave of delight hit me. My excitement was such that I slapped the back of the man in front of me. He fell to the ground from the impact. 'You prick' he whispered anxiously. 'I thought I had been shot, just as we got here!'

'Sorry, mate.' The huge grin belied the apologies. The Yanks smiled as, with a new_found lightness of step, we moved towards the warmth and welcome of Kotori and its tents with petrol heaters, its mess tents with hot food and, most of all, a place to sleep for ever in peace! Surely, this was the equivalent of entry to heaven! The emotional mix-up of safety, where one expected either maiming or death, the delight tempered with deep regret and uncertainty about the fate of close associates, caused the elation I felt to be a little muted. First, I wanted news and then sleep followed by food. They were my priorities. The limping Yank was led away by medical orderlies; he waved cheerfully to us. I have never discovered his name and didn't see him from that moment onwards. I sat waiting for food with my head clasped in my hands, my eyes closed, as I contemplated on my good fortune of the last three days. I was alive and in good health. Now I wanted to know about my mates, hopefully their fortune had been as good as mine.

After a quick mess tin meal of hash, which filled the corners of my stomach, I staggered away, with the other survivors and into a warm tent, crept into a newly issued sleeping bag fully clothed except for footwear, which I had the decency to remove, and lapsed into a long, deep, dreamless sleep. There was, of course, no news as to casualties in the battle, it was too soon and the situation was somewhat bemused, so sleep was victorious.

Many hours later I emerged sleepy-eyed, from the tent, to find to my delight, groups of green-bereted figures performing various chores. Sorting out what kit they had left, cleaning weapons and engaged in low conversations. There was none of the usual skylarking; all were serious of countenance. I eagerly joined in. To my dismay I discovered that of the 900 men that had set out with the relief force, only 400 returned. How many of the missing 500 were killed or captured it was impossible to elicit. I started to search for my own blokes. The Assault Engineer Section had consisted of 14 men at the outset. At this stage I found seven Marine survivors, which was more than I expected but terribly depressing. I was delighted to see the cheerful features of Polly Perkins, but of the small group I had been with he was the only one. Reuben Nicholls, Gerry Balchin, Lew Heard and Ray Ogle, of them there was no sign. The one aspect of the battle which was satisfying to hear was that the 400 survivors had accomplished the task and helped to bring out of Hagarui the trapped US Marine battalion, and all were back at Kotori. The remnants of the 1st US Marine Division was now all together and in one place. One tiny problem existed; the rest of the territory was now firmly in Chinese hands. The nearest allied territory was an enclave around the port of Hungnam which was hopefully to be the port of exit, because I had a feeling that perhaps we wouldn't be hanging about in North Korea for much longer! The tiny snag was that Hungnam was about 40 miles south-east, and between us and it was one road, through the vicious mountains, in deep winter with the temperatures even lower than ever. However, being a very tiny cog on a large wheel containing about 10,000 similar cogs, I was not alone, though I felt it!

As I sat quietly ruminating on the events of the past few days, I was aware of a far from subtle change in the atmosphere at Kotori. The élan which had been so self-evident among the marines of both nations had dissipated to a degree. All seemed to have faith in the eventual escape from our present predicament, but there was an undercurrent of anxiety which had not been present before. Two heart-stopping pieces of news did little to lift morale. One was that we were now completely surrounded by a large Chinese army. The second, that the road through the mountains had been blown up at a particularly vulnerable point.

A memorandum from the Yankee General caused a certain amount of glee, when it announced, 'The United States Marine Corps has never, in it's history, retreated in the face of the enemy. This tradition will not be broken on this occasion. As we are completely surrounded, whichever direction we travel will be an advance. Therefore, gentlemen, when we break out of here, we will be advancing to the south!'

One couldn't argue with the logic of this inspiring message, but the optimism announced as to the continuance of tradition may have stirred the blood of the Yanks, but wry derision amongst the Commandos.

The supply aircraft were still zooming over, disgorging supplies, most of which parachuted into the encampment, though some could be seen landing in the hills occupied by the Chinese. I sincerely hoped that all the delicious wholesome food was landing in our territory and the Chinese were receiving, with my blessing, all the fruit cocktail! Incidentally, upon my return to Kotori I examined the tin I had not consumed; it contained baked beans. This would have been definitely more filling than the fruit cocktail, but I knew that my circumstances were such, that had I consumed beans, my sphincter control would definitely have surrendered to the blandishments of the beans, which would have been embarrassing to say the least! Imagine being captured because the Chinese had been able to home in on noisy exhalations of anal wind!

CHAPTER FIFTEEN

Break Out

The main preoccupation in the period prior to the attempted breakout to Hungnam and safety was to keep warm and well fed. I was consumed with envy when Reg Higgs, the huge six-feet-plus marine, discovered that there was something amiss with one of his feet. He nipped off to the sick bay where the ailment was diagnosed as fairly severe frostbite. How he had managed to walk the distance he had was a miracle of perseverance. I envied him the fact that he would be airlifted out, particularly when we were informed that we would be marching the 40 miles to Hungnam! I toyed with exposing just my little toe to the elements to contract a similar ailment. This thought was rapidly discarded when I saw him being airlifted away. The casualty helicopters in those distant days were quite small machines. There was insufficient room inside for a stretcher casualty and, to overcome this difficulty, they had two stretcher pods attached to the outside of the helicopter, exposed to the elements. They looked singularly precarious, Reg's expression as the aircraft took off was such, that if the distance ahead of us had been 100 miles to be marched in bare feet, I wouldn't have changed places with him!

I knew the peaceful bliss of waiting for the off could not last for long. The discovery that we would be taking our turn on perimeter protection and reconnaissance wiped the smile from my face!

'Here we go again,' I thought, as I buckled on my equipment over the bulky layers of clothing. Darkness was descending and the temperature was 40 degrees below zero. There was a definite chill in the air. I had forgotten what it was to have comfortable warm feet and my lips had a permanent hard crust of chap. I grabbed a last cigarette which I enjoyed tremendously; cancer was the least of my worries at this time! Off we trudged towards the darkening hills. Christ, it was bloody cold. The snow was a frozen crust which crumbled noisily underfoot. The wind was piercing and we snuggled deeply into our warm parkas blindly following the man in front. Slungon my shoulder, I still possessed the rifle I had purloined from the dead Yankee. One of the party had a small mortar and the rest of us were further burdened with six mortar bombs each. We were to relieve a platoon of Yank marines on a prominent hill-top and, whilst there, keep observation on any possible Chinese movements and report by radio. The wind and snow now caused the situation to become distinctly arctic. I could hardly observe my own feet in the bad visibility, let alone marauding Chinamen! We passed through the outer perimeter of the Kotori defences and up the hill, through the scrub vegetation which was completely ice-bound. At last we arrived at our destination at the peak of the hill. The Yanks we were to relieve lingered not. As we arrived they were away like long dogs. So would I have done. It was absolutely ghastly. It was impossible to dig in, the ground was like armour plate. I wondered why the Yanks had not built a wind break. I was soon to discover why not, when my attempts, in the high wind, blew away my ambitious idea as fast as it dispersed the snow blocks I was attempting to manufacture. Sod it, it was impossible.

The mortar-men were setting up their little mortar. It looked rather futile when they had completed, a little pipe, facing skywards already icing over and about as much use as a eunuch in a brothel! We stood around, singularly unwarlike, stamping our feet and trying to keep the blood circulating. Visibility was virtually nil. One consolation was that the Chinese, however hardy they may be, wouldn't be too enthusiastic to play soldiers in such conditions. One report we had received earlier was that the Chinese were using camels to carry supplies forward to their lines. Camels? In this weather? I resist the use of the pun about them having the hump! We settled in for the night. Please, morning, come quickly!

'Dave, look what I've found.' The marine was carrying what looked like a bundle of icy rags in his arms.

'What is it?' I wasn't really very interested in anything except the cold.

'It's a dog. It just wandered in from the bush.'

I found it almost impossible to believe, but there it was. It looked like any hairy mongrel you would find roaming in an English street. It didn't even appear to be sorry for itself and was obviously well used to the horrible climate. The cheerful demeanour of the little mongrel in spite of the intense cold, which appeared to have no effect on the beast whatsoever, lightened our spirits. It became the focus of attention and helped to take our minds off our own discomfort and troubles. It wagged its icy tail at the slightest titbit from the 'C' rations which were thrown its way. We were working a two-hours-on–two-hours-off watch system. During the on-watch period the happy dog was good company, and it unfaithfully transferred its allegiance as the watches changed. During the two hours off I snuggled, fully clothed, zipped up tightly in the self-induced warmth of the sleeping bag, semi-conscious and almost contented. The circumstances became almost bearable. In the back of one's mind, however, whilst attempting to sleep, were the tales one had heard of the Chinese, creeping up on outposts such as ours and bayoneting the entrapped occupants of zipped-up sleeping bags. This knowledge caused the sleep to be shallow and I always awoke slightly jaded!

The freezing night wended its painfully slow journey towards the dawn. As the faint lightening of the dawn began to manifest itself, a ritual that has remained unchanged since the history of war began, on battlefields, we 'stood too' the dawn. The theory was that we should all be alert as the day dawned, as it was the ideal time to attack. We assumed warlike postures around our stupid little mortar. The Chinese, no doubt, were doing exactly the same thing; at least I hoped that they were. The thought of them, sallying forth, to do us all a terrible mischief, was unpleasant and caused me to grip my stolen rifle even tighter.

As morning, with its slight lift in temperature, began to cheer us up there was a build-up in tension, as sounds, almost disguised by the fierce wind, indicated the approach of a party of men. The dog, in an instant, lost its new-found popularity by barking a welcome to the oncoming group. The raucous barking faded away to a high pitched squeak as a marine kicked it firmly up the arse. From then on the dog was quiet and slightly less friendly. As the figures appeared out of the morning gloom and were recognised as US Marines, muzzles were lowered and safety catches applied. There was no conversation, no civilised pleasantries. We quickly picked up our mortar and scurried back down the hill with the same alacrity shown by the group we had relieved the previous evening. Alas, the little dog was left behind, presumably to enjoy the hospitality offered by the relief unit.

As I stumbled through the interminable snow, I pondered, with high expectations, a breakfast bulging with calories and carbohydrates, thick with grease and singularly unhealthy to normal society, who had the luxury of worrying about waist sizes and heart attacks. The breakfast to be followed, yet again, by a further few hours in the idyllic bliss of a sleeping bag. I looked no further than that. Life was being lived as it happened without contemplation as to future events which could perhaps be a little painful. I could not remember when I had last been refreshed and alert. With my mates, who were in exactly the same condition, tiredness and freezing temperatures had become the norm. I could now understand why Eskimos were seldom portrayed as jolly people. I wondered how they mustered the necessary enthusiasm to procreate under such conditions. I was reluctant to expose my frozen digit to urinate, never mind even consider its pleasurable activities! My mind was dulled by the cold and keeping alive and warm were the predominant ambitions. Still, not to worry, the next few hours promised the luxury of rest and warmth.

My elation was slightly diminished when, on our arrival at the British-occupied part of Kotori, I could see what was left of the unit, which was pitifully few, milling about fully kitted and ready to go. The roll call was taken, with far too many silences in response to names being called. We really had suffered rather grievously and lots of familiar faces were missing.

The whole encampment was a hive of activity. In one quiet corner of the enclave a bulldozer was busy excavating a large hole in the frozen ground. Beside the hole were rows of frozen bodies. One horrifying aspect of violent death in such climates was that the body tended to freeze in the attitude it had assumed at the time of death. Here were no neat lines of recumbent corpses carefully laid out. This courtesy was impossible due to the grotesque and pain-ridden positions of the sad men at the actual time of their demise. Dead frozen arms were stretched out in supplication, facial expressions revealed the terror, fright and anguish they had suffered. Some bodies were twisted unnaturally with the painful contortions of death. These sights were, for me, an indication of the failure of politicians to resolve national differences peacefully. It is a pity that the vast majority of them never actually see the results of their incompetence, ambition or greed. My deep sadness at the sight of these casualties, which could have produced, in me, pacifist tendencies, resulted in completely contrary emotions. I was, from then on, overcome with the desire that they should be avenged. I felt a rage and hatred for the little yellow men which the years have not dimmed. It is irrational but true. In the early 1980s I attended a Royal Tournament at Olympia in London. The visiting celebrity was the Chinese Defence Minister, dressed in the same drab uniform worn by the Chinese soldiers in Korea. He stood at his podium to take the salute. His uniform and his oriental features filled me with memories which produced intense feelings of hatred for him and his ilk!

As I gazed at the line of bodies in Kotori I noted, with a sense of shock, that I was gazing at a corpse dressed in a commando jacket. I reluctantly approached it, to find that the corpse was a Chinaman. He had obviously purloined the garment from a marine either captured or killed and had met his death whilst so attired. Time was of the essence, so without much delay, the bodies were interred. A military padre spoke a few short words, probably, because of the circumstances, his shortest ever sermon. As the plaintive bugle call *The Last Post* reverberated through the encampment, men stood silent and at attention, sad, respectful and grateful to be alive, as the bulldozer carefully refilled the large hole, hiding the obscene results of war and masking the bodies that would cause countless grief in little homes all over the world! With a sad shrug of my shoulders I turned my back on the scene and erased the sadness from my memory as I rejoined my mates.

I discovered, to my dismay, that my dreams of food and rest were only dreams after all. The First Division, United States Marine Corps, was about to advance to the south! Palls of smoke breezed into the chilled sky as stores and equipment were burned to prevent the Chinese from benefiting from our departure. The 40 miles to go seemed a long way, in the snow, on foot, but, as one Commando called out, hopefully, 'At least it's all downhill, mate!'

The cruising Yankee aircraft were busily bombing what foes they could find into oblivion. The roaring of their engines, the whoosh of their rockets and the indescribably ugly sound of their napalm, performed a constant background noise of hope for us on the ground. Whilst the warlike sounds continued they were keeping the hordes of Chinese on the defensive we would have a fairly even chance of escaping along the bolthole, the road to Hungnam.

In single file, spaced on each side of the dirt road, one side of which was hard against the steep slopes which looked down on it, and the other side overlooking steep gullies which led to misty snow-filled inhospitable valleys, we started our march to safety. Our vehicles had been destroyed and those who were incapable of marching had been transported to Hungnam by the busy little helicopters. The anonymity afforded the crushed dead on the road whilst we had travelled in our trucks no longer applied. We were walking on human beings, flat as pancakes, with familiarity easing the ghastliness of the situation and the desire to survive overcoming natural revulsion. As we marched, sluggish in defeat without the adrenaline of victory to ease our step, I was conscious, for the first time, of a sense of observing history in the making. I saw the lines of tired Marines, stretching as far as the eye could see, on the narrow frozen thoroughfare. Conversation was at a minimum, with minds and feet fixed on the task ahead. Icy wind and snow being driven horizontally into our faces increased the misery but at least we were heading in the right direction. The Royal Marine Commandos were withdrawing to safety after a defeat from a much superior enemy, the United States Marines were advancing against the foe . . . yet we were all travelling in the same direction!

Left, right, left, right . . . I retreated into my mind at the regular monotony of the march. Normally on a long march I habitually looked down at the ground just ahead of me and surrendered to my thoughts. On this occasion it was not possible because of the gruesome sights of the crushed soldiers, who, throughout history, had retreated in terrible weather with their morale shattered. I tried to compute the advantages I had over one of Napoleon's soldiers, during the retreat from Moscow. I came to the reluctant conclusion that I was much better off than he had been. This made me feel better. He had had no air cover of swarms of vicious aircraft, he was not as warmly clothed as we were and it would be an exaggeration to suggest that our morale was low . . . we were high because we knew we could get out! We were pissing off from what was probably the most inhospitable terrain on earth; certainly it was so bad that it wasn't really worth fighting for . . . I thought of my favourite expression, often used when things appeared to be not quite of the excellence I had hoped for, 'Fuck them all, except the cook, and fuck even him after dinner!' I smiled to myself and plodded on, with an ear cocked for the musical sounds of the Yankee air force burning Chinese before they could get close enough to me to be a personal nuisance. No, things weren't too bad after all. We might even make it!

The moment of high morale passed and I resumed the head-down slouching gait, which, as I looked around, was the general posture of the others. In spite of the background warlike noises there was a melancholy silence from the long shuffling lines of marines. The biting wind had eased slightly. For a brief moment I was able to raise my head without feeling the fierce pecks of driven snow blasting into my frozen face.

Astonishingly, the ungainly forward movements developed

for a brief moment, into a semblance of order and we were actually marching almost in step. A weak voice, somewhat uncertainly at first, but rapidly in strength, croaked, 'She's a big fat bastard, twice the size of me . . .'

I could not believe my ears, there was so little to sing about, but instinctively, in response I roared out, 'With hairs on her belly like the branches of a tree!'

I was not alone, the second line had been chanted, with considerable vigour by almost all of the Commandos. The words of the obscene song reverberated through the hills. The loud British accents echoed through the alien valleys, which would never hear the like again. The Yanks looked a little surprised. As I sang lustily my spirits rose. Our stooped and tired bodies straightened and our increase in morale was almost a visible emotion. I felt a tremendous pride in being part of such a group. If one can be jingoistic under such circumstances then one is unbeatable. Of course it could not last. Weariness quickly returned after the last wavering line of the song, 'And she goes to Church on Sunday,' faded away in shuffling misery. The temporary fillip of the song, did however remain as a warm inward glow which helped to sustain morale for a little while.

The painfully slow progress continued, with frequent stops as the rattle of small-arms fire indicated Chinese attempts to stem the escape of the Division. Such was the exhaustion that the whine of bullets, though not completely ignored, caused little reaction unless someone was actually knocked over. The people who caused me some amazement throughout the campaign were the medical orderlies. They were absolutely magnificent with a courage I could never hope to emulate. The commando medics were all matelots who had been seconded to the unit. They were completely untrained in commando tactics but gained the wholesale respect and admiration of the commandos through the whole operation. Here, even on the long march when their exhaustion was as complete as ours, they continued to operate. A far cry for them from their normal environment on the high seas! When casualties occurred on the Hungnam Road, there they were again ... magnificent.

We continued to snail our way towards the coast, our protective shell was the air force and our snail trail was the crushed bodies of the enemy and the recumbent figures of the newly killed escapees. At every enforced stop we collapsed on the frozen road, aware that each time we would have to painfully drag ourselves to our feet and start all over again.

At one such pause rumour swept through the ranks like wildfire, 'They have trucks waiting for us ahead, just a few miles to go.' We nodded wearily as the tale was told, perhaps it was true maybe not, but even the possibility, lurking in the background of the mind, helped a little to take just one more step. Every little helps, I thought, as the man said as he pissed in the sea!

For one brief moment I found that I was walking on slippery metal instead of frozen earth. I lifted my tired eyes and saw that I was on a prefabricated metal bridge over a short yawning gap. There was a drop of hundreds of feet below. I subsequently discovered that it was at this point that the Chinese had blown away a portion of the road where it had clung tentatively to a cliff face. The Yanks had, with the experience for which they are renowned, airdropped bits and pieces onto the narrow road and in spite of heavy casualties had succeeded in bridging the gap. The engineering skill display in this operation was beyond belief. Had they not accomplished this seemingly impossible task all would have been lost, because there was no way round.

The light dimmed, night fell and with it the temperature. We marched, stopped, marched and stopped, occasionally coming under fire. We were sustained in our endeavours by the consistent rumour that trucks were just around the next bend. They never were, but they might have been! Apart from the appalling tiredness, we were now suffering from severe pangs of hunger. For hour after hour we stumbled through the night and as the dawn appeared we were still plodding along. An indication of the new levels of weariness we were suffering was the appearance of various items of personal equipment scattered on the road surface, having been discarded by the exhausted marines. Packs, entrenching tools and helmets, sad and abandoned, rested on the road. I even saw one or two sleeping bag rolls . . . foolish! Though bulky they were not heavy and if things became worse without the warmth of a bag, one could die. Even more serious was that if, as was likely, it was purloined by a Chinaman, it would help him survive.

As dawn arrived on the third day of the march I was completely knackered and ravenously hungry. We were as unsteady as a gaggle of drunken sailors returning from shore leave. I was so pleased, yet again, to have the long rifle as opposed to a short carbine, for I was now using it as a sort of crutch. It was helping to keep me on my feet. Something was different; my befuddled mind took a little while to sort it out. Then I realised that I was travelling on level ground, not downhill any more. The threatening hills, when I searched for them with bloodshot eyes, were gone. The land was generally flat, though undulating slightly. Ahead I thought I could hear the sound of cheering. Hallucination time I thought, yet another step in my deterioration. I crested a gentle slope feeling more than sorry for myself and my mates. Again a ragged cheer from ahead. I felt the smarting sting of tears in my eyes as they focused on the magnificent view ahead. There, as far as the eyes could see, were line after line of beautiful American trucks. We had made it! I tried to cheer but choked on the attempt. I felt tremendous sadness for my mates who were not here to share this moment, but who lay dead, back in the hills. I felt a tremendous gratitude for the Yanks whom I had castigated in the past, they really had surpassed themselves in getting us out. I was brought back to reality when the tears that ran down my cheeks promptly froze amongst the whiskers on my face.

CHAPTER SIXTEEN

Escape to Tokyo

Using the last vestige of my strength I clambered over the tailboard of a truck and collapsed in a heap on the cold metal floor, surrounded by my exhausted mates. The vibration of the truck as it moved off was the psychological equivalent of manna from heaven. The singing noise made by the heavy military tyres on the frozen surface matched the singing of my heart. I have never since felt the release of tension so vehemently. My eyes closed for the first time in 72 hours as I lapsed into pleasant uncaring unconsciousness.

My tired mind was forced into wakefulness by a combination of shouts and movements. A message from my nose forced my heavy eyelids reluctantly open . . . food . . . food, I could smell food. My twitching nose dragged me to my feet. In my tiredness I could see and hear again the obese jolly cook from the USS *Perch* calling out, 'For you . . . for you.'

I shook my head to clear my mind. The galley of the submarine disappeared as I joined the other marines in the queue for food. We were all staring fixated at the steaming dixies of food. Our concentration was that of a beast of prey poised before its victim. I was transfixed with the sight and sound of the steaming stew. At long last my mess tins were brimming with grub and with a steaming mug of hot coffee. I scurried away to a corner. I guarded the utensils with my hands and would have cheerfully killed, with my bare hands, anyone foolish enough to attempt to take them from me. I scoffed the lot. Large mouthfuls of sustenance were crammed into a mouth overflowing with food. The gravy dribbled down my chin . . . Henry the Eighth at his most nauseous would have been proud of me. As I belched loudly I felt the warmth of the food spread through my body . . . bliss! As my stomach rumbled its thanks I was aware that the temperatures at these lower altitudes were higher than those in the hills but it was still bloody cold. I was made aware of the difference when the gravy on my chin did not freeze solid, and the area was a sea of deep chocolate-coloured mud!

The welcoming lines of tents beckoned to us. Outside each tent was a large drum of petrol, the pipe that ran from the tank led into the tent where it fed a carburettored heater, glowing red. We fell into the sauna-type atmosphere and slid into our sleeping bags. Now that there was no fear of attack I securely zipped up the bag and cocooned from the cruel outside world, slept like the dead for hour after hour. Much later, fully rested and refreshed, we gathered outside out tents and for the first time were informed as to our casualties. One had only to look around to realise how few remained. 'Sticky' Baines, the RSM with a heart, broke the news that of the 200 of us who had started out, 45 where killed or missing and 34 had been wounded, which made our casualty rate almost 50 per cent. I felt sick. Of course I was relieved to have been lucky enough to survive, but I remembered that if I had not met Percy and his lot at the time of lowest ebb, I too would have been a casualty statistic. I was pleased and delighted to spot my 'runashore' mates, Gerry Maill and Bill Taylor amongst the survivors. I thought that none of us would ever be the same again.

'What's the date?' I asked.

No one knew. A voice from the group of marines, after

obviously using his fingers as an abacus, called, 'The 11th of December.'

I thought to myself that the last fortnight had just flown, or had it? We had just received our first mail from home. I read the spidery handwriting of my mother in which she had evinced some anxiety as to my safety. I would write to her soon and relieve her worry, but not yet. I could not marshall lucid thoughts and would not relax until we had left this godforsaken country.

The next morning we gathered together our pitifully few possessions and lined up hopefully as the same amphibious Amtracks in which we had travelled a short 19 days before, rumbled alongside us, and we embarked. We were leaving. Within days we were steaming south along the east coast of Korea in a large US Navy transport called *General G.M. Randall*. Hungnam was now evacuated and that portion of North Korea, which had been the scene of victorious joy some weeks earlier, as the Marines had advanced against negligible opposition, was now firmly back in Chinese hands. I leaned over the rails of the troopship, sadly remembering the missing faces, congratulating myself on my survival and far from eager ever to see Korea again. The tranquillity of the sea journey was disturbed and brought us crashing back to reality when we paraded for a burial service of those Yanks who had made it back to Hungnam and had then, sadly, succumbed to their injuries. As, to the pious words of the Marine Chaplain, they slid from under their national flag and disappeared beneath the waves, I felt that their grave was infinitely preferable to those unfortunates interred on the wintry plain of Kotori.

The same Chaplain who had conducted the burial service was preaching to church services on board, which were packed with survivors, giving thanks. I left after a few minutes. I was safe now. For the moment I did not need Him. My main priority, at the moment, was not God, though I might need Him again at a later date, my main need was a hectic shore run, with Bill and Jerry, with a copious supply of all the necessary equipment for application to all the known vices and lots of ale to drown my sorrows should I become maudlin!

There was much speculation as to our destination. The epitome of delight would be to travel back to Camp McGill at Yokosuka with its useful proximity to the delights of Tokyo. Our questions were answered when the ship slowly steamed into a port bustling with much military traffic . . . No luck, not Japan, but shit and derision! The Port of Pusan on the extreme south-east tip of . . . Korea! From Pusan we moved to a town called Masan, some miles away. It consisted of a large camp with the familiar USMC tents and was clearly designed to allow us to rest and recuperate. The tents were boarded at the base and contained comfortable bunks. It was here at last, that I met my first Korean civilians. The women of Masan were amazingly ugly, probably the ugliest women in the world; the men stocky and morose. I could not help but remember that the Korean men were used, in large numbers, as POW guards during the Second World War and their cruelty was legendary. I was dozing on my bunk one sunny afternoon when, outside, I heard piping voices singing softly, 'London Bridge is falling down, falling down, falling down'. I staggered outside and there were half a dozen quaint Korean kids singing away in almost unrecognisable English. They were extremely cute and somehow managed, in spite of their squat faces and narrow eyes, to convey wide-eyed innocence. Deep down though, even their youth could not conceal the natural ugliness of their race.

Masan was a small town which had been overwhelmed by the recuperating licentious soldiery. One discovery made whilst drunk, was that their primitive sewage system could be extremely dangerous. Their lavatories consisted of a fairly large deep hole in the ground, with foot shaped blocks of compressed mud on either side of the aperture. The danger was that a misplaced foot could easily slip into the deep hole, causing agony closely resembling that of a rupture, or the victim, for one pain-ridden moment resembled Long John Silver – minus parrot. The stay at Masan was fairly short but enabled us to regain our taste and appetite for good food, plenty of beer and, if one was either blind or not too fussy, to re-establish our sexual ability with women, who started the evening looking like a female version of Boris Karloff and culminated, under the influence of much alcohol as beautiful as the Mona Lisa!

We were finally informed that after the period of rest and recuperation we were going to resume our original role as a raiding unit and were being transferred to Admiral Joy's Raiding Forces forthwith . . . good news!

While we were digesting the good news that we would be returning to independent operations once more, a rumour buzzed through the ranks that some of our blokes, who had been taken prisoner in the Kotori battle, were going to be allowed to broadcast from Peking Radio. Though such activity was discouraged by the Marines, who could blame them? It would be their way of letting their folks back home know that they were alive and well. I would have wanted to do the same had I been a prisoner.

As the evening of the broadcast arrived we grouped anxiously beside the radio. We would be pleased to hear as to who had survived the terrible winter in the hands of the Chinese. We were subsequently to discover that many of our lads were to die in captivity and that the others were to have to wait for almost four years before they were repatriated, a terrible experience for them. We who had escaped were indeed lucky!

The start of the broadcast was greeted with a deeply emotional but silent concentration from the assembled marines. We were relieved as the simple family messages revealed to us the names of our mates, whom we had presumed to be dead, coupled with the information, from them, that they were being reasonably treated. We were not quite naive enough to believe the latter. I was pleased for their families; at last they would know.

Then came a bitter shock which left us stunned with disbelief. A Marine Condron came on the air. I did not know him personally, to me he was just a name. He commenced his message, as had the others, with a statement as to his health and the reasonable conditions under which he was living. Then to our absolute amazement, at the conclusion of his personal message he commenced a diatribe regarding British involvement in the Korean War and regaled his Chinese captors with praise. He propounded the Chinese point of view as to why they had entered the war. Sad emotion turned to anger as his short message was broadcast. When it came to light, years later as to how the rest of the captured commandos had suffered, many to the point of death, I felt it shameful, to the ultimate degree, that he should have behaved in what seemed, at the time, to be such a traitorous manner. At the conclusion of serious hostilities on the peninsular of Korea when the time came to release prisoners, he was the only British POW to move to China and live. He stayed for many years but eventually returned to the United Kingdom.

A sequel to this shameful episode occurred many years later, in 1986, when a reunion was arranged at the Commando Training Centre at Lympstone in Devon. This reunion was a few months prior to Prince Edward bottling out and retiring defeated from the Commando School. On my arrival, full of anticipation at the thoughts of meeting old friends from over 30 years away, I learned to my amazement, that Condron was present. The organisers of the reunion pleaded with those of us, and there were many, who objected to his presence, not to create an atmosphere. As this was only the second reunion in over 35 years, we agreed rather than mar the occasion. The ravages of time were clearly etched on our lined faces. We were greyer of hair and thicker of girth. We cast aside the controversy regarding Condron's presence and wallowed in our memories as we attempted, aided by copious quantities of ale, with some success, to recapture the élan we had possessed in our youth. Nevertheless Condron's appearance rankled as we discussed, behind his back, our distaste at his presence after what had seemed, all those years ago, his lack of loyalty to say the least. Reluctantly I had to admit to myself that he was a large impressive figure, tall and distinguished in appearance and conducting himself with dignity in the face of ill-concealed hostility of the group ill disposed to him.

After the reunion I felt a compulsion to write to him and state openly my opinions rather than have left it at back-slanging. I felt I owed it to my mates who had died in confinement to tell him of my hostility. This I did. My letter, very direct and polite, informed him that I would much sooner have seen at the reunion those prisoners of war who had not gone over to the Chinese but who had died unsung in captivity. His reply was immensely detailed and polite, his vocabulary wide and his disagreement with my opinion vehement. He detailed his account of the trials and tribulations suffered by himself and the other prisoners. He did not elucidate as to his reasons for going to China from captivity rather than return with the POWs but the tales he told of the life he had led and explaining that he was responsible for the well-being of a number of the prisoners by his attitude, coupled with the harrowing descriptions of the life under the Chinese, caused me some second thoughts. His denial of collaboration was sincere. I reasoned with myself that not having suffered a quarter as much as he had as a prisoner of war, who was I to pontificate? Who was I to believe that given the same dreadful circumstances I would have behaved differently? Much as I had, thought the years abhorred this behaviour through lack of knowledge, his demeanour placed a lingering doubt in my mind. However, at the time of the broadcast, with the information then available his attitude on the radio was immensely demoralising as we shuffled out to continue the war.

There was an element of sadness involved in our departure from the US Marines. They were, without doubt the best of the American armed forces and we had been through sticky times with them, but commando troops are trained for and at their best when engaged in small clandestine operations. The retreat of the UN forces in which we had been involved from North Korea had re-established the importance of the east coast supply line to the Chinese People's Army. It was time, once again, to turn our back on land warfare, return to the sea, and land behind the lines to give the North Korean railway system some more individual attention. If we worked really hard at our task we might even bring it down to the standard of the British Railway system at home. When we had reached that pinnacle of accomplishment, then they, the Koreans would really be in trouble! Our last night in Masan was spent in the self-entertainment of a 'sods-opera'. In the open space besides our tents the beer flowed and voices were raised in obscene songs to the accompaniment of the plink of Binnie Barnes's banjo. Huge quantities of steaks and chops were barbecued and consumed. We left our Yankee comrades the following day, distended of belly, thick of head and sad of heart! The past was behind us now and we were ready and fairly eager which was accentuated by the desire to revenge the 72 men who were no longer with us since the unpleasant days at Hagaru and Kotori.

Happily among the survivors were my mates Bill Taylor and Gerry Maill. Gerry was to be awarded the American Bronze Star for some mischief he had caused a large number of

Chinese, with his machine gun, and was more than willing to expound on the incident at the drop of a hat! On our return to the land of the rising sun, we were sent for a week to an Australian-run centre at Ebisu very near the centre of Tokyo. It was a superb place with unlimited supplies of beer, baccy and bumf! By about the fifth day of our week's posting, we were sated with beer and fairly skint financially, having had quite an expensive week which had mostly been spent in the vicinity of the 'Ginza' where the fleshpots of Tokyo then were. Gerry had, one afternoon, leaving behind the waft of his acrid pipe tobacco, disappeared to we knew not where. Bill and I sat in deep comfortable armchairs in the large room the three of us shared. I was quite exhausted but determined to continue our fling for as long as possible. Bill looked terrible, his bloodshot eyes peeped from a lined and worn face. He had looked infinitely fresher after the Hagaru battle, and he had claimed to be completely knackered then!

'Well, Bill,' my hoarse voice a merest croak above a whisper, 'we are skint, we need money for tonight.'

'Have you got anything to flog, dear boy?' The usual suffix 'dear boy' was the norm in any conversation with Bill.

'No I haven't, have you?'

'Not a bloody penny, absolutely skint!'

In the ensuing deep silence my mind was racing to produce an answer to our predicament. The Japanese were extremely friendly as a race at this time, but the friendship tended to evaporate like urine on a hot pavement if one was broke! Suddenly I sat up, my eyes brightened and I wallowed in a self-congratulatory sense of genius. I leaned towards Bill and carefully observed over both shoulders that what I was about to impart would not be overheard. I whispered, 'Gerry was boasting that he had two parkas, wasn't he?'

'He was indeed.'

Our eyes pivoted, like compass needles springing to the north, and settled on the open door of Gerry's locker. There, hanging luxuriously, was a superb example of American cold weather equipment a fur-lined parka, much sought after by all and sundry.

'No one should have two of those,' I greedily smiled. 'We'll flog one of his, get pissed with him tonight, then break the news to him that his extra parka has financed us, okay?'

'What an excellent idea, dear boy.'

In a flash the room was vacant, the only indication as to our previous conversation being an empty coathanger, gently swinging to and fro from the impetus of our hasty removal of the expensive garment!

Fifteen minutes later we returned to the room, 10,000 yen better off. This was about £10 sterling, more than enough for a good night out at contemporary prices, which, in 1951, were very low! With a guilty start I pushed Gerry's door closed rather than have the empty hanger, now still, gaze at me ruefully at the singular lack of comradeship I had displayed. In an attempt to justify the evil act I had just performed I comforted myself that it really was Gerry's fault; he should not have boasted regarding his possession of the extra parka. There was now a need for rest, to prepare us for the future evening's entertainment. A gentle 40 winks was called for, but before I finally dropped off, I could hear Bill's snores vibrating the window panes, indicating that his conscience was troubling him not one iota!

I awoke as Gerry wandered into the room. He was whistling happily whilst still smoking his pipe, a rare feat!

'Come on then lads, ashore we go.' His eyes twinkled, 'Don't worry about money. I've got hold of a little, enough for a few beers anyway.'

'Off we go then, dear boys.' Bill was awake. 'I'll just have three esses and we'll be off.'

'Three esses?' the expression was new to me.

'Yes, a shit, a shower and a shampoo.' He strolled off to the bathroom guffawing at his witticism.

Shortly afterwards, spruced and smelling of three pox doctors' clerks, we sallied forth to enjoy the delights of Tokyo. Many, many pints later, all of which had been paid for by Gerry and slightly guilty about the unspent 10,000 yen bulging my pocket, curiosity overcame me,

'Where's all the money come from, Gerry?'

'It's got absolutely fuck all to do with you,' drunkenness made him quite obscene.

Bill looked at him through half-closed eyes, his speech more than a little slurred, 'You been selling your body, Gerry?' as he raised his glass and took a mighty swallow of the Asahi beer.

'No. Alright I'll tell you then.' He looked from one to the other, triumphantly.

'Remember my spare parka? Well I flogged it!'

With a strangled watery gasp Bill spurted beer all over the table and then began to choke. I slapped his back to ease his torment. Our eyes met and we collapsed in helpless roars of laughter.

'What's up with you stupid bastards?' Gerry looked puzzled, as well he might, because he was going to be bloody cold when we went back to North Korea!

At about the same time, in a nearby bar, 20 surviving members of 'B' Troop of the Commando were engaged in a celebratory drink. It was suggested to them, by a nearby group of American soldiers, that it would be better that they should be over the water, in Korea, earning their keep by fighting, instead of skulking in the back areas of Japan. To be fair to the Yanks they had just returned themselves, but it might have been a good idea had they made some enquiries before embarking on such a foolhardy endeavour. This was, understandably, resented by the marines, one of whom, appointing as his personal target, a large vociferous American Infantryman, engaged him in a *tour de force* which bore very little resemblance to the Marquis of Queensbury's rules. This proved to be too much for the assembled spectators from both sides, and so they joined in. A magnificent fracas developed. The result was that the Yanks were forcibly expelled from the Japanese Inn. The proprietor, as always called frantically for the military police and, as an afterthought, ambulances. Though all was far from amicable, no further blood was spilled whilst negotiations progressed, until, with a singular lack of thought an over- excited MP drew his service pistol in an attempt to induce the commandos to evacuate the premises. He was disarmed and, it was alleged afterwards, unsuccessful attempts were made to place the barrel of the pistol into one of his orifices which was not designed to accept it without considerable pain.

The situation had now deteriorated to 'considerably dicey!' The arrival of two Australian military policemen resolved the situation. With typical antipodean aplomb they approached the slightly irate marines. 'Oi mates, we were in the middle of a game of cards. Why don't you all fuck off home, then we can go back and finish our game?'

This earthy approach caused a roar of laughter from the bedraggled marines where upon, to the surprise of the Yankee MPs, the members of 'B' Troop did what had been suggested so succinctly and went peacefully back to their billets.

Meanwhile, one of the unit's cooks, a large man, as befitted one whose occupation allowed him the pick of the unit's food, was quietly drinking on his own in yet another Japanese hostelry. He always drank alone and was renowned as an amiable giant who was completely imperturbable. If he had an Achilles heel which could disturb his equilibrium in an instant, it was to be addressed as 'Limey'. He considered this a somewhat derogatory label and it made him very, very angry. At an adjoining table were a quartet of friendly American sailors.

One was heard to say, 'I'm going to buy the Limey a drink, I like Limeys.'

The cook glowered at him through lowered eyelashes. His scowling demeanour did not deter the friendly Yank, who slapped the cook soundly on the shoulder and with a friendly smile, drawled, 'I wanna buy you a drink Limey – okay, whatcha drinking?'

'Don't call me Limey!' red of face and breathing heavily.

'Come on Limey don't be a sourpuss, have a drink.'

A huge fist blotted out the vision of the undeserving Yank as the cook went noisily berserk.

Some little while later the cook found himself severely pinioned, in a straight-jacket, at the American stockade. An American Medical Officer approached tentatively and looked down at the quiet Marine on the floor. 'You okay now?'

The cook, very still, nodded that he was. He had now recovered from what, to him, was a deadly insult. All was forgotten and forgiven as far as he was concerned.

The officer turned to a nearby MP, 'The Limey's calm now, unstrap him.'

Neither of them noticed, unfortunately, that the word 'Limey' had caused the cook's complexion to change to a deep puce! As the straps were unbuckled, the cook glared at the Lieutenant with undisguised hostility.

'You behave yourself now, Limey. You are amongst friends here.' The officer spoke in friendly placatory tones. As the last buckle was released, the MP stood back, his task complete.

With a roar the cook shook himself free of the untied jacket and launched himself at the officer. 'Don't call me Limey!' he roared as his ham fist struck the unfortunate lieutenant on the nose!

Back at Ebisu the watchman gazed, in amazement as Rex Swancott, the very large frogman, lurched towards the entrance. He was slightly in his cups and was dressed, from head to foot, in full Australian Army regalia. He was not able, even when sober, to explain where he had obtained the garments, or how. Somewhere in Tokyo, a large Australian was in a somewhat similar situation as he was fully clothed as a Royal Marine Commando. The mystery was never solved.

The following day, as reports from various parts of Tokyo, as to the happenings the night before began to permeate through to the powers that be, they seemed quite upset! It was decided that the Commando should be banished from the fair city of Tokyo, and thus it was that, without preamble, we found ourselves, in the blink of an eye, under canvas at Kure, many miles from Tokyo, never to return! How we suffered, because in an attempt to burn off all the excessive energy we seemed to possess, we embarked on a training schedule which was obviously designed not only to keep us fit but to knacker us so completely that aggrieve sorties to nearby towns were out of the question!

Time progressed, the winter temperatures dissipated and it was time, we thought, to start our operations against the Chinese. As though they had read our minds, we were assembled in a large hall, and when the usual phalanx of officers appeared together we knew that this indicated a briefing for an operation.

Duggie gathered the whole unit around him and we sat on the floor agog for information. The gen he imparted was good. For the first time, instead of operations by small segments of the unit in the dark, using rubber boats, we were going to land, as a complete unit, not too far south of the Russian border in daylight, and we were going to stay ashore for eight hours and do their railway system a really decent mischief. A happy buzz of conversation rippled through the assembled commandos. This was home territory to us, what we had been trained for and what we could do well.

As Duggie continued, the cheerful bustle of conversation was stilled, and a chilly silence ensued when he revealed that the intelligence had indicated that the Chinese were aware that something was afoot. This had probably resulted from loose talk at the dockyard, where the ships for the foray were being prepared. Duggie stated that, in view of the leak, he had considered cancelling the operation but had, however, after much thought, decided to go ahead. He urged us to keep quiet about the impending raid. This news caused us to be a little subdued but not for long. We were now eager for the off, the sooner the better.

CHAPTER SEVENTEEN

Sonjin to Hiroshima

In the days that followed, Percy briefed us as to our role. We were to destroy a large railway embankment not too far south of a large communist supply depot. The railway appeared, on the embankment, briefly between two tunnel entrances and near the beach. It was about 200 yards long, 40 feet high and of similar width. It had been shelled and bombed to no avail and seemed impervious to that form of attack. We were not, at this stage, given the name of the target area or its location. We, did however, spend many hours perusing aerial photographs to familiarise ourselves as to the task ahead. There were no culverts which would have eased our task; I was grateful for this having an aversion to paddling through Korean crap for the second time! We would have to burrow in from the top in a large number of places so that the main charges, many tons of explosives, could be set, deep down, for the maximum effect. We could not use mechanical equipment to dig because of the terrain and could not do it manually because of the time element. Percy had decided to use shaped charges, called beehives, to blast the holes for the main charges. These charges fired lumps of molten steel deep into the earth and made the necessary holes. They were ever so noisy, so the quiet approach was out! We all knew the techniques and were well trained in the method.

It had been established that there was a North Korean fishing village abutting the embankment on the landward side. I sincerely hoped that the operations would not destroy the homes of these innocent villagers. One consolation was that they would probably hide in the tunnels whilst the operation was progressing and we would not cause them too much physical harm. I had absolutely no qualms about damaging oriental soldiery but drew the line, very much, at the possibility of hurting innocent women and children.

At last we were off to the docks, the unit now at full strength, the casualties having been replaced by commandos seconded from the brigade in Milaya. I remembered my original surprise at the USS *Perch*. It was as nothing compared to my first sight of the USS *Fort Marion*. It was an ugly ship of strange design, which mystified me until I was informed that it was specifically designed to launch Amtraks, the amphibious armoured vehicles in which we had embarked at Hungnam months before. These craft were extremely heavy, too heavy to be launched by hoisting outboard from davits like conventional landing craft. The drill with them was to embark the assault troops in the Amtraks whilst they were still on board, in a well deck which was an open compartment on the ship. Instead of lifting the craft off the *Fort Marion*, it was flooded and sunk by the bows. As the mother ship filled with water, the Amtraks floated off and when they were clear the *Fort Marion* was pumped dry and the bow rose again to the surface. All very clever, I hope it works! Then we received some good news. On normal small raids the raiding parties all landed together; on this occasion there would be two waves of assault troops and we the assault engineers, because of the immense quantities of high explosive we would be carrying, were to be relegated to the second wave. An even better bonus was that we would be travelling in conventional landing craft and not the unstable Amtraks. This was to facilitate the unloading of the explosives down a ramp and directly onto the beach. Every cloud does have a silver lining! It was slightly unusual to perform a commando-type raid, some 150 miles behind the enemy front line and so close to the Russian border, in daylight. We would be particularly vulnerable over the eight-hour period of the operation, therefore it was with some relief that we were told that an American naval force would accompany us, consisting of the US Cruiser *Saint Paul;* her eight-inch guns would be some consolation if things went haywire. With her a number of American destroyers would sail and we would all be protected by our old friends the American Air Force. Who we knew, from past experience, were fairly expert at keeping an enthusiastic enemy at bay. It did not really look too bad. In fairly good spirits we started to load the stores and explosives for the operation. I was puzzled to note that among the impedimenta were boxes of anti-personnel mines. Why, I wondered?

As we settled in to our cramped billets aboard ship the convoy set sail. I looked down at the gathered Japanese workers on the jetty as the gap widened between the awkward-looking assault ship and the pier. I wondered which of the undemonstrative bastards was likely to spill the beans as to our departure. The engines throbbed as we steamed out of harbour. It was comforting to look across the calm sea at the accompanying flotilla of support ships. A far cry from one submarine and six rubber boats. Instead of the usual 40 or so of us, at least the whole unit would be involved.

At last the target location was revealed to us as a beach about 80 miles south of the coastal and supply town of Sonjin, 150 miles north of the 38th parallel, which was the current front line between the United Nations Army and the Chinese. A very long way to walk if we missed the boat. Morale was high. Duggie, who was very popular with the lower deck, visited the various troop areas and with practised ease became reacquainted with the survivors of Chosin and established his usual rapport with the newer members of the Commando, who had replaced our missed mates. It was a constant source of amazement that troops of such élan, who were capable of creating merry hell in their leisure moments, who were trained to use personal initiative when it was required, were kept so firmly under control at times such as these. Probably it was because of the mutual respect engendered between the marines and the governors. We had much faith in one another, unlike the Royal Navy where the class barriers were so firmly adhered to that the average rating despised his seniors and was probably right to do so.

Whilst on board, control was emphasised by the constant piping of the loudspeaker system, the interminable repetition of, 'Now here this, now here this,' followed by strings of instructions to various factions of the organisation. We were told when to eat, where to eat, where to go, where to sleep, when to wake. The constant humming of ventilation fans and the protesting creaks of steel bulkheads as the heavy ship ploughed through the seas, all combined to disturb the relaxation of the commandos as they sat about, playing cards, inventing rumours or simply trying to get some sleep. Two days and nights elapsed. There was no noticeable tension as a body. But I found myself mixed emotionally. My eagerness to avenge my dead mates was tempered with a desire to survive. The onset of gnawing doubts deep inside me, the usual physical reaction to events about to unfold. As I leaned over the rail, deep in thought, I attempted to philosophise how I felt personally about war. It is easy for intellectuals to marshal lucid thoughts on a subject about which they could be unemotional because of actual nonparticipation. To the soldier, such as myself, with little formal education, it came a little harder. Here I was, with a group of men about to land on an alien shore, kill people to whom I had borne no ill will prior to the war. I was sailing, perhaps, towards another nightmare of torn flesh and the cries of hideous pain from brother human beings. Why? There is an excitement about the thought of war. The preconceived ideas engendered by a youth which had been jingoised by the sound of military music, which I love, the waving of flags and the exhortations of patriotism. These could easily be induced when one was protecting one's own homeland, but how on earth could I put myself in such jeopardy for someone else's territory? As the busy sea bustled past the steel sides of the ship, I gazed, hypnotised and never did rationalise my thoughts. It boiled down, I supposed, to the ability of the politicians to con the lower stratas of society into these extreme behaviour patterns. Once I realised that I had been well and truly conned, as had we all, I thought no more about it. Anyway, it was too late, it had become personal now. I wanted to avenge those commandos who were always going to rest in the cold ground around Kotori. I shrugged my shoulders, put the pitiful attempt at philosophy behind me and decided to get pissed as soon as we returned from this foray!

Dawn on the third morning of the journey, the rattling of anchor chains indicated our arrival. The ship hove to as we readied ourselves for the raid. A thick sea mist hid us from the shore. I was pleased, but my pleasure evaporated when I realised that the same mist would make the provision of air support not only difficult but well nigh impossible.

We had been awakened in the early hours and were rigged in our warlike regalia. I spotted Bill Taylor on the deck and wandered across to him. 'Pity the weather is reasonably warm, eh Bill?' I smiled weakly.

'Why?'

'Gerry hasn't got a parka!'

We both chortled at the thought.

'How are you feeling, Bill?'

'Don't ask me, dear boy. Have a fag.'

We had, since being roused, been smoking cigarettes to an alarming degree. My mouth tasted like a sewer and the anxiety in my stomach grew as the time to land grew closer.

'See you later, Bill.' I raised an arm and wandered back up to my group, we were to be in different landing craft.

The landing craft were swung out and lowered to the surface of a gently swelling sea. At least it was calm, because in rough weather the flat-bottomed boats tended to become unstable and induce sea sickness. It seems a little unwarlike to stagger ashore green of face and vomiting. The calm waters were, therefore, a little bonus. I could hear the Amtraks making the most incredible noise as they floated slowly away from the mother craft, they wouldn't be a lot of use on a night raid, too bloody noisy!

As I clambered down the scrambling net to the bobbing landing craft, a tremendous crash caused me to drop the remaining 20 feet or so in record time. As I landed breathless with shock, I felt that a heart pacemaker would be a good idea as an item of personal equipment. The crash was the first broadside from the USS *Saint Paul*. The shells whooshed overhead through the mist, to be followed, after a pause, by the menacing rumble as the shells exploded on the shore. I hoped the villagers would have time to reach the safety of the tunnels. Our craft began to circle. This was normal procedure, the circle performed by the landing craft as they waited for all of the wave to arrive was known as the war dance. As soon as the convoy was complete they would line abreast and head for the shore. The Amtraks of the first wave had already been swallowed up by the fog as they headed towards the target. Bill was in an adjoining landing craft. I caught a glimpse of his white face peering over the side at me. I gazed back at him equally wan. We both raised our eyebrows to heaven and he puffed furiously at his cigarette. I envied him his smoke; it wouldn't have been a good idea for me to do so at the time, I was sitting on tons of high explosive. I thought that if the enemy didn't get Bill and me, then nicotine certainly would!

As we headed into the shoreline the cruisers and destroyers were blazing away in a crescendo of noise. Through the mist I could hear the tap-tap-tap of the heavy machine guns on the Amtraks as they approached the shore. I felt uncomfortable that we should be making so much noise. It was so alien to our normal approach. Usually the first the enemy knew of our presence was when he was sitting surprised, in a pool of his own blood. This way of doing things was blatant and unsubtle! There did not seem to be any return fire from the beach, which was as probably as well because we were almost engulfed in box after box of high explosive. I groaned as I looked at it because every last ounce would have to be manhandled all the way to the target.

'Stand by to beach.' This from the American coxswain.

'Down ramp.' He shouted to be heard over the warlike noises caused by his compatriots in the large ships astern of us. The wires sang through the pulleys and, with a crash, the lip of the ramp hit the beach.

'Out troops.' This order was in a British accent and we scurried over the ramp and out of the craft ready to throw ourselves prone should the necessity arise. Beach? This was no beach, it was a collection of huge rocks, difficult to clamber over. The shell-fire moved inland as we disembarked. Quickly we carted our beehive charges across the rocky beach and up the huge railway embankment. The mist swirled and the skies were silent. No aircraft!

Under Percy's directions we placed beehives at about eight-yard intervals and joined them together with detonating cord until they were united in a ring main like Christmas tree lights.

I took the opportunity to glance at the village on the other side. My heart sank when I saw that some of the poor hovels were roofless and damaged. I also noted that a gaggle of villagers were being led into one of the tunnels to safety. At least the women and children were, the apparently able-bodied men were searched and questioned before being similarly put under guard. Within a little while, all was ready for the first bang. As the first assault wave of commandos had passed through the village, the head man was spoken to, through an interpreter. He informed them that a large body of Chinese soldiers had passed through the day before, heading north. He took the commandos to a hut which the Chinese had used as temporary headquarters. There amongst the debris left behind was a map of the immediate coastline region. On the map was drawn a big red arrow, pointing from seaward to a beach two and a half miles north of our present location. Someone had indeed spoken out of turn, and they were not far out! However, if there was a Chinese force waiting at that beach, it shouldn't take them too long to cover the short distance and put in an unwelcome appearance. With a blast from a whistle for the benefit of the commandos, and a cry of 'Fire in the hole!' for the Americans with us, an enormous explosion resounded through the hills as the first layer of beehives drilled deep holes into the solid embankment.

Shortly after the explosion a crowd of Korean civilians were seen approaching the perimeter from the north. A commando left the hole he had dug and approached them. As he did so they suddenly scattered and a group of Chinese soldiers opened fire. They had been shielded by the civvies. The marine flew back into his trench unscathed and a fire-fight ensued during which the Chinese withdrew, carrying their wounded with them. There was no doubt that the enemy were aware of our presence and we worked that wee bit faster than before; it was apparent that they would return in much greater numbers.

More bangs from more beehive charges enlarged the holes and we worked like beavers delving into the embankment. The mist began to lift, as did our spirits, because now the Air Force could join in the little game! Providing they resisted the desire to bomb us, all should be well. Almost six hours elapsed since the landing, and at last, we finally began to pack into the holes the huge quantities of explosives. Noting the proximity of the village and relating it to the amount of explosives that we were using, I had to admit to myself, reluctantly, that its chance of unscathed survival was minimal. I felt a terrible regret which stayed with me for a long time. I had seen them: they appeared to be simple fishermen and their families, with, apart from their houses, not much else. They probably just wanted to get on with their lives and didn't give a monkey's who ruled them. This, to me, was a really sad aspect of war.

The blasts of whistles and cries of 'Fire in the hole!' caused us to stand up and gaze skywards, for what goes up, must nearly always come down! In this case, the lumps would be large and heavy. The explosion was tremendous and completely obliterated the railway and embankment along its visible length of about 200 yards. Percy had, as usual, done his sums right! As the dust settled, the area was a complete shambles. At this stage the presence of the anti-personnel mines became apparent. One reason that the Chinese didn't mind too much if the damage was minimal was that they had an unlimited supply of manpower and could repair material damage in remarkably swift time. To discourage this it was decided that anti-personnel mines would certainly delay the repair project. All over the shattered soil, engineers were digging little holes; alongside each hole was placed a mine. The metal cylinder had a narrow metal collar protruding from the top. From this collar protruded three prongs. They were to be buried until only the tip of the prongs protruded above the ground. The slightest touch on one of the prongs would cause the mine to leap about four feet into the air whereupon it would explode and cause terrible injuries to anyone nearby. It would certainly delay repairs by the Chinese army. I didn't mind that they should never have joined. I was perturbed, however, about the villagers. As those of us deputed to arm the mines placed them carefully into the prepared holes, covered them gently with soil and then removed the pins, the portion of ground became untenable. In answer to my concern about the villagers we were told that the headman would be informed and told to keep them off. I had sleepless nights over that one; had they told him? I wonder to this day!

At about the same time as the outer perimeter of commandos were beginning to withdraw in preparation for disembarkation, the radios began to buzz with the gen that a large formation of Chinese troops was heading towards the beachhead. Though our task was completed we still had to get away unharmed if possible. Withdrawal was almost as hazardous an enterprise as an actual landing, if the enemy were about, so it was with considerable relief that we cheered a flight of US Navy planes as they sped, at low altitude, towards the oncoming enemy. The distant sound of bombing shortly afterwards indicated that the Chinese had been discovered. We scampered back aboard our landing craft and disappeared towards the fleet floating offshore. We left behind a decimated fishing village, frightened and confused civilians and a railway system which would take a very long time to repair. From a logistical point of view the raid was a success and would inconvenience the forward-supply situation for the Chinese, but I still, all these years later, hope and pray that the Korean women and children did not roam, out of curiosity, over the demolished railway embankment. A slight consolation was that the villagers had been left an ample supply of food by the commandos, to tide them over the difficult days ahead.

Once again we sailed south though, happily on this occasion, no young men wrapped in weighted hessian slid from beneath their national flag into the sea. We had been singularly fortunate, thanks to good planning and Percy's expertise, we had done it again. On our return to Kure we settled into our old routine: booze, crumpet and lots and lots of training, hopefully to keep us in an exhausted and relatively safe condition!

It was during this sojourn that I decided to visit the city of Hiroshima. Although some five years had elapsed since the dropping of the atomic bomb on the city, I felt the need to see the place, not with the inquisitiveness of a tourist, but out of genuine desire to see and remember in the future, the extreme limits to which man can descend in the name of politics. As I arrived at the tidy but devastated city I felt a sense of awe. Here, thousands and thousands of people had died in seconds. The debris was all gone, but the wide open spaces remained. The atmosphere was that of cathedral-like sombreness. There was silence, even though the town was slowly returning to as near normal as it would ever be again. I felt a nervousness within me, a feeling that I did not want to linger, that it had been a mistake to come here. I analysed my emotions as that of not wanting to be thought of by the locals as a ghoul, like the eagerly curious spectators who gather at a serious accident and who almost slobber with the excitement of it all. I had to get away from the sad-eyed locals, and I did, quickly. Though my stay was for a very little while, the atmosphere at Hiroshima is a memory that I would choose to forget. As, at the time the atomic bomb was dropped, I was on a troopship heading for the Far East, I had always delighted in my strong support of using the monstrosity, as it had probably saved my life and millions of others in a similar situation. Had I not visited the city my emotions would have remained unaltered. I am still glad that, at the time of the decision was taken, they did drop the bomb . . . I think! I wish fervently that I had left Hiroshima out of my itinerary!

The weeks progressed through May and June of 1951. We had been a long time in Japan on this occasion and I fondly hoped, with the lack of activity, that the powers that be had forgotten our very existence and that we were going to sit out the war in peace. On the mainland of Korea the war had settled on or about the 38th parallel, in a stalemate of trench-type warfare. There was little we could do there, what had they in mind for us? We were soon to find out.

As July approached I could sense the usual signs of activity among the higher strata of our society that things were afoot. Sure enough, we were once again gathered together, the usual 'break ranks' as we gathered around Duggie and his cohort of officers. The intelligence officer removed the white sheet from the blackboard; underneath was a large-scale map. It showed a bay, an inlet in the East coast of Korea. In the south-west corner of the harbour was the town of Wonsan. In the actual harbour were a smattering of very small islands, some eight or nine in number. The islands were almost completely surrounded by the mainland shore. Duggie smiled, reached for a wooden pointer, the tip of which he tapped again and again against the little islands as he spoke.

'This is the harbour and city of Wonsan, about 70 or so miles north of the 38th parallel. It is an important military centre and there are many Chinese units stationed there. Our task is quite simple really, in the near future we are going to infiltrate ourselves on to these islands.' The pointer tapped on the board. 'Once we are established we will occupy the islands, with a small detachment of South Korean marines, and harry the enemy from there. We will probably stay for about six months. The enemy will be quite anxious about our presence when they discover us, as they surely will. Their anxiety will be occasioned because they will never know whether or not we are a prelude to a full-scale invasion as happened last year at Inchon. The US Navy maintain that they can supply us and keep the Chinese from attempting to regain the islands from the sea. One of the islands is a leper colony; don't worry about that, the MO tells me that leprosy can only be contracted by close and long-term contact with the lepers.'

There was a stunned silence from the assembled commandos.

CHAPTER EIGHTEEN

Wonsan Bay

Once again we were on a Yankee transport ship, heading north up the Sea of Japan, with the hills of Korea to the west. The situation ashore as far as the war was concerned was that the United Nations army and the Chinese were now established, in great strength, along defensive lines at the 38th parallel. Stalemate had developed territorially, though fierce battles were being fought, reminiscent of the massive assaults of the First World War. Ironically the armies were in almost the exact positions occupied by the opposing sides at the start of the war. Absolutely nothing had been gained by either side at the cost of tens of thousands dead!

Our morale was very high; we were on our way some 70 miles north of all the frenzied activity, on our own, to create as much mayhem and inconvenience as we could! Lovely!

We learned, on route, that Wonsan harbour was a fairly large enclosed bay about 10 miles deep with an entrance about 5 miles wide between two peninsulas. The main island, Yodo, was about three-quarters of a mile square and situated at the mouth of the harbour between the necks of the two peninsulas. There were about eight or so other smaller islands inside the harbour, much smaller than Yodo and much nearer the Chinese occupied mainland, some thousand yards from the shore. We were to establish ourselves on Yodo and then gradually infiltrate all the other islands and take them over. Once we had done this we could then start making a bloody nuisance of ourselves by doing the Chinese considerable naughties at every available opportunity.

Due to the proximity of the enemy most of our operations would take place at night. This suited us tremendously because this was what we had been trained for and were quite good at. We had, of course, to avoid face-to-face confrontation, because the Chinese could probably muster considerably more than the hundred or so of us. It would be, if we did it wrong, as though Popeye were attacking Bluto without the benefit of spinach! The Yanks had assured us that they had swept the harbour clear of mines and that there would be constant destroyer presence, to prevent the Chinese doing to us what we intended to do to them! Travelling with us were a number of Koreans, dressed in their national civilian dress. They were members of the various intelligence agencies. Their activities were none of our concern. They would also be resident on our little islands and would wander off on occasions to perform their nefarious activities! I did not like them much and kept away from them.

As we sailed through the dark Korean night the indication of our arrival was the stopping of our engines. The usual clamber down the scrambling nets and into the landing craft that was no novelty. The muted rumble of the diesel engines and we were on our way. I was always fascinated by the degree of fluorescence in the waters surrounding Korea and this night was no exception. The scenery, in the half light was delightful. The humps of the looming mainland hills were the usual beautiful purple colour. I could appreciate the beauty on this occasion, as we were not actually going to land on the attractive mainland. The other reason for approaching the oncoming landing with courageous calm, was the knowledge that, the night before, 'C' Troop with some of Lieutenant Thomas's Heavy Weapons, including my old mate Bill Taylor, had landed and dealt with the very light opposition ashore. I have never landed so bravely; what a difference it makes if some other silly sod has already taken all the risks. I wish that all landings were thus!

We stumbled ashore on Yodo. The beaches were of a fine sand and the vegetation, as far as one could ascertain in the gloom, appeared lush. The island was very hilly and in more peaceful times would have been a paradise to holiday on. As we stumbled inland, there erected, in sheltered hollows, out of sight, were tents. We rapidly divested ourselves of our heavy loads and were led to defensive positions overlooking the sea, for the usual dawn 'stand to'. As the summer sun rushed over the horizon it illuminated a view that I will long remember. The sea was a shimmering blue, unpolluted and beautiful. Dotted here and there were small islands. Overlooking the whole sight was the dark shadow of the mainland, looming from three sides, with the Sea of Japan stretching behind us. Unbelievable was the presence of the three American destroyers, cruising the narrow waters between us and the Chinese-infested mainland. If I were Chinese I would have considered their presence a diabolical liberty.

The peaceful scene was completely unrealistic when one considered it from a combat point of view. However, the illusion lasted for only a few brief moments. The Yankee ships suddenly went down at the stern and their bow waves increased as they circled and accelerated. I watched, puzzled at their sudden manoeuvres. All became clear as I noticed harmless-looking cascades of sea water appear around them, to be followed shortly after by the sharp boom of artillery from the mainland. The ships performed what we came to know as their 'war dance'; their guns replied and the erstwhile idyllic scene was transformed as, over the horizon, from seaward a low-flying flight of US Navy aircraft roared towards the mainland. The Chinese artillery ceased firing immediately as the shoreline became hazy from the smoke occasioned by the rockets launched from the American aircraft. The Yankee planes flew lazily out to sea to recommence their patrol. The destroyers eased back to cruising speed. The Chinese went back to their breakfast noodles. All was transformed, in the twinkling of an eye, to the scenic beauty of before. The token dawn chorus of war had satisfied the egos of all concerned. Peace prevailed! Our introduction to the strange situation over and having left sentries to keep observation of the situation, we retired to our tented hollows to settle in for the unrealistic days and months that loomed ahead.

The first task was to reconnoitre the island and dig defences in case the Chinese were, at some stage, able to avoid the marauding destroyers and get to us on the island. The two-man slit trenches were soon established and fire lanes cleared. On the highest peak of the island, which offered an unrestricted view of the entire bay, was dug a deep latrine. Instead of the rough isometric bars providing the seating we produced a number of boxes with a bum shaped hole put in the top. These were placed over the latrine pits and offered not only unrivalled comfort whilst performing in the summer heat, but also an unrestricted view of the entire bay. One could sit there for hours with a pair of binoculars and watch the war going on, with the added advantage that, if the situation turned nasty, one's orifice was perched over an aperture which would allow one to vent one's fear without embarrassment or mess!

Some small detachments of Korean Marines were established on the small island nearer the shore. However, one island, Hwangto-do, called by our marines the endearing name of 'Wanky-do', had been attacked by the Chinese and they had recaptured the island from the South Koreans. This was to be rectified by us later. The South Koreans from Wanky-do had withdrawn to an island called Sin-do and the leper colony at Tae-do. This colony was, by mutual consent, left alone by the combatants. One morning, the South Korean noticed that a large steel canister had floated ashore on the adjacent small island. It was too close for comfort if it were a sea mine and they requested that it be dealt with.

At that particular time I was the only engineer NCO on the island.

'Ah Corporal. They have a problem at Sin-do.' This cheerful message from the troop commander at Yodo.

'What's that, sir?' I asked, radiating confidence.

'They have a bloody great sea mine washed ashore nearby. You are to go and deal with it.'

My heart stopped. I knew as much about sea mines as I did about brain surgery. My confident smile faded and my knees sounded to me like a long burst of machine gun fire.

'I know sweet fuck-all about sea mines, sir.' I gazed at him hopefully, thinking that he might delegate the task to the US Navy.

'I'll get a pamphlet sent over. Be ready for the off tonight.' He wandered off, happily leaving behind a somewhat confused and frightened alleged commando. Some short hours later, a grey covered pamphlet was thrown into my billet. I had griped and complained about the situation to my mates and they welcomed the arrival of the book with noisy laughter. I toyed with delegating the task to one of my marines, but that wasn't on, not out of any loyalty to them, but because of the knowledge that should Percy hear of my dereliction he would tear me up for arse paper! So I kitted up and readied myself for the nauseous exercise.

I crept off to a quiet corner and perused the pamphlet. I toyed with the idea of reading whilst on the hilltop toilet but this would have caused so much ridicule that I abandoned the idea. The book contained details of dozens of infernal devices, each one more frightening than the one before. There was little I could do until I had seen the bloody thing, so I tucked the book away for future reference.

I forced my trembling body to walk towards the beach for the appointed time. There, floating gently in the tide was a ramshackle old assault craft that had seen better days. The crew were South Koreans, some in civvies and others in uniform. It was apparently a night-time ferry between the occupied islands. I was the only European on board. I was unhappy! At the last moment two Yank soldiers appeared. They were apparently the liaison between the Korean mercenaries and Allied forces.

'Hi. You the guy for the sea mine?'

'Yes,' I gulped attempting to display *savoir faire*.

'We'll drop you off on the island and collect you after dark tomorrow, okay?'

'That's fine,' I mumbled as the news got worse and worse.

I looked casually around to see if there were any lifejackets on board, there were not. I settled myself aboard and, with a shattering roar with the occasional bang of a misfire, the engine drew the craft from the clutches of the beach and we headed off, noisily, in the dark. I unslung the two packs of explosives from around my shoulders and rested them at my feet. The craft, I thought, was either going to sink or get lost. Either way I was in trouble. I displayed the outward calm that the two Yanks were showing. If they travelled like this for a living they were obviously complete nut cases. However, they evinced no anxiety whatsoever.

As the night progressed we beached on a couple of occasions and disgorged Korean occupants, I had not a clue as to our location. Eventually the engine slowed and one of the Yanks, the more cheerful of the two, therefore obviously a psychopath, called across, 'Here you are fellah, see you this evening, okay?'

I tumbled ashore and with a heart-rending roar the craft moved astern and disappeared into the night. I sat there, surrounded by my paraphernalia of destruction. I felt quite lonely. I sincerely hoped that I had forgotten nothing because it was too late now.

The dawn slowly crept in, lighting up my surroundings and allowing me to introduce myself to the little island. It was almost only a sand bar, one consolation was that a fairly large island, by comparison, was about half a mile away and another the same distance in the opposite direction. Which one was the abode of the South Korean Marines and which one the leper colony was my only problem. I commenced what I hoped was a casual stroll around the short beach line of the tiny island.

'Christ, oh bloody hell!' My eyes were like a racing dog's goolies as they alighted upon the object of my presence upon this stupid sand bank. It was a huge steel cylinder about five feet long and about three feet in diameter. I looked in vain for the horns that most sea mines have as appendages; this had none. My limited knowledge then indicated that if it were indeed a sea mine, and if it had no horns, then it was either actuated acoustically or magnetically. My dilemma was that I didn't know how much noise, or how much magnetism would activate the thing. I flicked through the pamphlet for guidance, nothing to help me answer what I thought was a fairly important question. Page by page I flicked through the book, sitting by the infernal machine. Suddenly there it was, a photograph. I eagerly scanned the details. It was indeed a mine, a Russian one to boot. It was acoustically operated. My condition was such that I sincerely hoped that a terrified fart would not be sufficient to do the business. I tiptoed towards it to find that it had a fair amount of what I assumed to be Russian script scrawled on the casing.

The next and probably quite important piece of information I required was the amount of explosive contained within. There was no way I could be further than 250 yards from it because that was all the island that I possessed. I was still relatively unhappy. Included in the details regarding the mine was the information that it contained 240 pounds of explosive. This surprised me, the casing must be inordinately thick. I searched somewhat apprehensively, for an indication as to the position of the switch which would actuate the bloody thing. 'Percy, where are you?' I thought to myself. Ah, there was a cover plate, well rusted and immovable. It was just as well, because I didn't intend to move it anyway. As I was alone, any carefree bull about being unconcerned would have been wasted. I enjoyed the luxury of displaying my fearful emotions unobserved. I positioned one of my packs of explosives carefully against the plate, deciding to save the second pack for another go if it all went wrong. I knotted one end of my steel reel of electric cable to a stake that I had pushed into the ground and unreeled the wire as I walked away from the mine, relaxing visibly as the distance between me and 'it' increased. With a jerk the cable was fully extended. 'Christ that's a little too close still.' I was now talking out loud, to nobody; my bottle must indeed have gone! Still, with only 240 pounds of explosive to contend with and providing I dug myself in below the surface level, I should be okay I hope.

I dug frantically with my little entrenching shovel and produced a hollow, which, as I lay prone in it, would ensure that no part of my lovely and valuable body, would protrude above surface level. I nodded with satisfaction at the hole in the ground. My smugness evaporated as I looked towards the mine. 'Dear oh dear,' I thought. A gentle breeze stirred the scrub vegetation which covered that part of the island that was not sand. I looked towards the mainland, swarming with Chinese just beyond the adjacent island. I felt really rather lonely!

I reluctantly moved back to the metal monster. I was sure that it smiled sardonically at me. It was a mute opponent, with the capability of a roar of triumph at any moment. I was an expert at land-orientated explosive devices and doubtless a naval expert, aware of the capabilities and sensitivity of the mine , would have thought it a mundane exercise, but I was fumbling in the darkness of lack of knowledge and wished myself elsewhere.

I carefully affixed an electric detonator to the explosive cord hanging from the pack, joined the detonator wires to my electric cable and wandered back to my little haven, the hole in the ground. Whilst prone, but before settling in, I raised my head like a stoat seeking a rabbit. All was quiet. I attached the cable wires to the little machine which was to push the electric current along the cable and to the detonator, at a twist of a handle. I took a deep breath. My bottle went completely when I realised that I had placed, in the hole with me, the spare pack of explosive...silly me. I loped some 20 yards away and deposited the lethal package onto the ground and back to my hole.

I closed my eyes, snuggled into mother earth and twisted the hand grip. As the whirr of the generator died away there was a brief silent pause, which, to me, seemed to last about an hour. Suddenly there was the most tremendous explosion. The ground heaved beneath me. I tried frantically to burrow deeper, but my little hole discarded me with the alacrity of a bullet from a gun. Debris fell and projectiles pinged past me as I flew through the air. I was engulfed in black smoke and petrified with fear. As I fell to the ground a short distance from my hole, I shouted at the pamphlet writer, '240 pounds? You lying bastard!' I staggered to my feet, coughing and spluttering . . . if the Egyptian could see me now, he would have fallen about. There was smoke everywhere. What scrub vegetation had survived the blast was burning. I had a sneaking feeling that I had displayed my presence on the island, to friend and foe alike. Miraculously I was unhurt. Hundreds of birds on the adjoining islands were squawking and fluttering about. The crater formed by the explosion was immense. I could not tell the depth because it had rapidly filled with sea water. I sat on the beach, the island burning behind me, surprised that all was so quiet. An hour later a landing craft appeared from around the seaward island and headed towards me. I couldn't hear the engine, neither when they jumped ashore, could I hear any of the conversation of the commandos. I was aware that they were laughing. Some days later, when my hearing improved, I was informed that the explosion was so huge that they were sure that I had done myself a mischief and risked a daylight journey in the landing craft to pick up the pieces. Nowhere was there more hilarity than amongst my brother assault engineers, when we made the startling discovery that the pamphlet had contained a misprint and the true total of explosive was not 240 pounds, but 2,400. The charge is inordinately big because the mine does not actually touch its target, being acoustic, but attacks from a distance. If I could have got hold of the printer of the pamphlet I would have carefully castrated him.

CHAPTER NINETEEN

Gilhoully's Brew

"Tis about time we had a little drink up . . . what do you think, Dave?' The soft Irish accent woke me from my reverie. The large thick set man with heavy-rimmed spectacles and a beaming smile, slipped quietly into my bivouac. His enthusiasm apparent.

'What a good idea, Gilhouly. But where is the booze coming from?'

'I can fix that, Dave.'

'What do you mean, you can fix it?' I was puzzled by his confidence because alcohol was absolutely unobtainable and unlawful under our warlike island conditions.

'Well,' he paused for a moment, tapping the side of his nose with his forefinger, 'you just leave it to me. Come over to the sick bay at about nine tonight.' His self-satisfied smile lingered for a while after he had gone, raising my spirits at the thought of a wee drink. His disappearance was as unobtrusive as his entrance had been. Gilhoully was the Petty Officer medic attached to the Commando. He did like a drink and the enforced teetotal existence was, obviously, beginning to pall.

I had been day dreaming, mooning at my laundry that was bubbling away in a charred and blackened bucket. The boiling water causing my clothing to loose both dirt and its shape. The ignition for the dhobi was supplied by a small quantity of flame-thrower fuel, napalm. It produced a fierce flame and rapid heat which was an advantage; the disadvantages however, were the clouds of acrid smoke that it coated the outside of the bucket, including the rim, with a gooey black tarry residue which had crusted with constant use.

I sat cross-legged, gazing at the fire, contented. Reaching into my pack I produced a wooden Japanese flute. It was my habit in quieter moments to produce mournful tunes, which reverberated over the island. My mates hated it intensely, not only the music, but also my rendition thereof. Their dislike was so intense that in the past, on a number of occasions, I had returned to my bivouac and found my beloved musical instrument shattered beyond repair by an unknown, unsympathetic, music hater. However, I had had the foresight, aware as to my limitations as a musician, to purchase as a job lot, a dozen flutes, which meant that their joy at the destruction was short lived. Whilst they revelled in blessed silence, I would produce a new flute and start all over again, completely ignoring the cries of, 'Oh, no!' from surrounding bivouacs. I thought that perhaps, one day, the strain would be too much for them and murder would perhaps be committed.

At nine o'clock the same evening I wandered across to the sick bay dugout. It was a beautiful tropical night, the war being temporarily in abeyance. The crickets were chirping and I could clearly hear the rustle of the surf as it ebbed and flowed on the nearby sandy beach. Commando sentries were alert and watching the sea from their slit trenches, as with eager anticipation I approached the hanging blanket which served as a door at the entrance to the dugout. Pushing aside the blanket I entered. The place was thick with tobacco smoke and somewhat of a party was taking place with six Marines and a couple of medics in attendance. They were squatting about on the floor, with the light from the oil lamps reflecting on the glasses in their grubby fists. Through the tobacco smoke I could discern the rich disinfectant and familiar hospital aroma.

'Come in Dave, come in.' The cheerful voice of Gilhoully was slightly slurred, his eyes just the tiniest bit glazed. On a low makeshift table beside him was a large green tin of US navy-issue grapefruit juice. Beside the can were two pint bottles of clear fluid.

'Have a drink, son.'

'What is it?'

Gilhoully explained, at some length, and with considerable difficulty due to his fragile condition, that the bottles contained surgical spirit, which was used for sterilisation purposes. He further explained that a very carefully measured mix of one part surgical spirit to five parts of grapefruit juice was an adequate and safe drink, providing that the ratios were carefully maintained.

'I've heard that that stuff can blind you,' I said anxiously.

'Not in the hands of an expert.' He hiccoughed and held himself upright by grasping the table. 'I am an expert, so have confidence and have a bloody drink!'

'What the hell,' I thought. 'He should know.'

I picked up a glass, which I saw was a measure for medicine and took a tentative sip. The burning liquid tore at my throat, demolished it and performed the same service to the lining of my stomach. I engaged in a fierce paroxysm of coughing and was in considerable distress.

'Good eh?' shouted Gilhoully proudly.

'Yeah, good,' I spluttered, my eyes watering. The rest of the party nodded in agreement. The second drink was imbibed with much less violent a reaction from my internal organs and I settled, with the others, into garbled conversation with company which grew more pleasant as time and booze progressed. One by one, as the evening drew on, the other guests wandered off, pale of complexion and quite unsteady gait. At one stage we had seriously thought of taking a boat and giving the Chinese aright good hiding, hoping to return to the plaudits of our companions, but, after a violent argument as to the venue of the proposed raid, the subject, thank Christ, was dropped.

'Time to go, Paddy,' I slurred, as I stumbled to my feet. I felt really quite ill. I had the almost irresistible urge to vomit and felt the possible onset of acute dysentery.

'Oil see yah back to your billet, Dave,' from Gilhoully.

'So will I.' I was unable to focus on the face of the second speaker, to me he was anonymous. We staggered through the night to my hole.

'Give us a tune then.' Gilhoully passed my flute across to me. As I placed the instrument of torture for others, to my lips, my body at last revolted against the poison within. I rushed clear of my bed space, unbelting my trousers as I did so.

'Here, use this,' from the unidentifiable marine. As my now bare bum settled on the receptacle so thoughtfully provided, things just did not feel right.

Through my misery, as I evacuated through every aperture, I could hear Gilhoully whispering in my ear, 'It's all right Dave, you won't go blind,' there was a long pause, he continued, 'I think.'

Merciful oblivion overcame me as I sank into happy, carefree darkness.

The coma cleared, I opened my eyes, blinking with the combined agonies of bright sunlight and a searing headache. As I slowly regained consciousness, memories of the night before flooded back. I cursed my abject stupidity for imbibing such a vicious concoction as proffered by Gilhoully. I moaned about my throbbing head, I exulted over the fact that I had not become blind. The overwhelming emotion, however, was puzzlement because there was definitely something amiss with my buttocks. I staggered to my feet, now somewhat frightened, grabbed my shaving mirror and, with some considerable difficulty, contorted my body so that I could see, in the reflection in the mirror, my nether regions.

'Oh no!' I blanched with horror. The pristine cheeks were sullied. A large circle of a blackish substance, crusty and vile, adhered to my flesh. Realisation dawned in a flash when I noticed that the radius of the circle was exactly that of the rim of my laundry bucket. The mark was a layer of old crusty flame-thrower fuel. I was scarred with napalm!

'I wonder if it's still flammable,' I thought, as I remembered the undignified moments of the night before, when I had been placed, unceremoniously, on the bucket!

'Gilhoully!' I roared. The panic in my voice, and the degree of urgency implied caused not only Gilhoully to come running, but also half the unit. Any sympathy which may have been lurking as to my plight was rapidly dispelled at the sight of my bum, pointing accusingly at Gilhoully. It was too much for the assembled Commandos. The Chinese on the mainland must have looked enquiringly at one another at the roars of hysterical laughter booming across Wonsan Bay.

The concern in Gilhoully's eyes, peering through his thick glasses, did not match his smile, as, with cotton wool and various substances including the same surgical spirit that was the cause of my present indignity, he attempted to remove the offensive residue to no avail.

'Can't get it off, Dave.' His voice broke with emotion.

'Keep trying you bastard!'

'I am, I am.' There was a hint of desperation in his voice. Exhausted he stood up. 'It's no good, you will have to wait for it to wear off.' The audience collapsed in deeper convulsions of loud joy, as I, red of face and rectum, began to panic as the substance began to sting. My hangover and aching head were forgotten because of the trauma at the other end of my body.

'For Christ's sake do something,' my wheedling voice pleaded with Gilhoully.

His smile faded. 'You'll have to go for treatment.' His serious demeanour caused my panic to grow.

Each day, a landing craft, when required, was used to take casualties out to a US destroyer, part of the war dance team. I was ushered down to the beach where the ill, injured and wounded from the previous 24 hours were awaiting the journey to succour and the release from pain. I joined them. The casualties of war were being joined by a casualty of extreme stupidity.

As the craft bobbed against the steel side of the destroyer, the immobile casualties were winched aboard, to be followed by the walking wounded. They were mostly South Koreans so I was spared the agony of describing the reasons for my presence to them. But the team of waiting medics on the deck of the destroyer were a different kettle of fish.

As I reached the upper deck an anxious-looking navy 'medic' took my arm and with deep sympathy said, 'Where did you get it, fellah? What's the trouble?' Around me the scene was busy as casualties were receiving medical treatment. I felt a terrible shame sweep over me.

'It's my arse,' I whispered, anxious not to be overheard.

'I can't hear you, boy,' from the understanding Yank.

'It's my arse.' I raised my voice a little.

'Your arse?' the Yank roared. His voice boomed across the deck, causing a slight stirring of interest from the assembled crew. The following moments are shameful memories, as, with scarcely concealed laughter, a group of medics and a Yankee medical officer first sighted my now painful ailment. The officer tentatively touched the obscene, painful crust.

'Do you know what it is?'

'Yes, it's napalm,' I mumbled.

'Napalm? How in hell did it get there?' he pointed.

'From a bucket.'

This reply caused a number of eyebrows to raise in astonishment. After a dramatic pause, the doctor spoke. 'Are they dropping it in buckets now?' He was struggling not to laugh. I was not amused.

With some difficulty I regaled the assembled and slightly disbelieving Yanks with my sad tale, as, with equal difficulty he managed to remove the majority of the substance. We were being constantly interrupted by various members of the ship's company. A particularly obnoxious little medic had self appointed himself as spokesman, as, with mounting delight, he repeated the story to each and every visitor. If I had been armed I would probably have shot him!

'You will have to wait for the rest to wear off,' said the medical officer in the same tone of resignation as previously used by Gilhoully, when he offered exactly the same consolation.

My humiliation was complete as a bevy of grinning sailors bade me farewell, as the craft pulled away from the destroyer and headed back to the island. I cheered up considerably, when, soon after leaving the ship, it began a war dance in response to the attentions of a Chinese shore battery. As the destroyer weaved and dodged I shouted, 'That'll teach you bastards to mock the afflicted!' They were, however, much too busy to hear my loud insults. I looked forward to telling Gilhoully what he could do with his moonshine in future.

During my stay on Yodo I cultivated the devoted friendship of a small, humpty backed, dwarf Korean pig. There were a number of them on the island apparently left there by the civilian islanders who had been displaced by the war. I grew very fond of this little pig and fed it regularly, and as a result it was constantly in the vicinity of my bivouac. It was disgustingly and untruly rumoured that its affection for me was so obvious as to be bestial, probably fuelled by my continuous compliments of its little curly tail. I completely ignored all this vile slander.

On one occasion when our supplies were lost after one of the landing craft sank, we were short of rations for a while. The cook produced a great stew from our scant and depleted store of food, which we all thoroughly enjoyed. It was shortly afterwards I realised that 'Curly Tail' was missing. I searched the island in vain, until the cook, with slightly tearful eye, announced that due some small administrative error, he had actually cooked my little friend. When he blurted out that we, including me, had eaten the unfortunate 'Curly Tail', I chased the cook all over the island. I mourned for a while but in retrospect, realised that the little pig had tasted rather good and forgave the cook in return for double rations for a week. My weakness seems to be my sentimentality.

CHAPTER TWENTY

Goodbye Binnie

As time progressed the Commando slipped unceremoniously ashore and quietly took over most of the small islands within the harbour of Wonsan. The Chinese were, by now, in no doubt as to our presence. We would, on occasions, engage them with mortar fire from the nearest islands and there was an almost constant procession of raiding parties. Our role had changed slightly; we were still aggression orientated, but instead of raids by as many as 60 commandos at a time, smaller parties, sometimes as few as four marines were involved. I was not nearly as busy. The railway, which had been our prime target for so long, did run some miles inland at this point, much too far away for our operations from the beaches.

After Gilhoully, the enthusiasm for an occasional little drink evaporated rather rapidly, much faster than did the brown ring of napalm on my bum! However, we still engaged in sober 'sods operas,' not quite as satisfactory as the drunken kind, but at least a morale booster for us all. As ever, the prime movers in the organisation of this self-entertainment were Binnie Barnes, the banjo man, George Maloney and myself. We settled in to a fairly satisfactory routine with the odd moments of excitement of a raid or two on the enemy shore to keep us contented and the Chinese on their toes. It came as a tremendous blow, when, one morning, after a night of small raids, harrying the Chinese, I heard the sad news that Binnie Barnes and Lieutenant Harwood had both been killed during one of the raids. We had been so long without serious casualties since the terrible debacle of the Chinese intervention that I had hoped, unrealistically, that our good fortune would continue. One never becomes blasé about death, even in an environment where death is never far away. Many good mates who had gone were frequently remembered. The emotions engendered had slightly eased with the passage of time, but the sadness occasionally surged inside me, unfortunately coupled with the selfish relief at my own survival.

With the other members of the garrison of Yodo I paraded for the military funeral of Binnie and Lieutenant Harwood. As the poignant notes of the 'Last Post' echoed over the island, I could almost hear the gentle tones of a softly-playing banjo behind the trembling bugle call. The emotional impact of the ceremony caused me an overwhelming sadness and a slight hint of moisture formed in my eyes dimming my vision. In my mind's eye I could see the slender lieutenant and the large figure of Binnie, a flamboyant, happy man quick to smile. Alas they were no more. It was all so bloody futile that my sadness changed to a quiet rage. I was a professional marine, it was a life that I had chosen. Death, or the prospect of death, had been a constant companion gnawing at the vitals for many a year now. One's most precious possession is life. One result of the death syndrome was to cause me to be even more jingoistic. I was immensely proud of the blokes with whom I served and of the country that spawned them. It is very easy to denigrate jingoism when you have no experience to draw upon.

CHAPTER TWENTY-ONE

The Little Chinese Gun

On the mainland, the nearest island being Modo, occupied by 'B' Troop of the Commando, was a little Chinese field gun which was becoming a pain in the arse, not only to the commandos on the island, but also to the American destroyers that were patrolling the straits between the islands. It was obviously hidden somewhere in a cave and would pop its snout out, let go a few rounds and then retract inside its hole and wait. The Yanks had blasted away with their destroyer's main armament, to no avail. The Yankee air force had blasted the vicinity into oblivion, but as soon as they departed, 'pop!' the little gun would open fire again.

I spent happy hours sitting near the hillside toilet, with binoculars gazing contentedly at the discomfiture of the US Navy at this cheeky bastard. Then it occurred to me, that, should the Yanks be unable to silence the bloody thing, they may want us to do it for them! The humour dropped right out of the situation immediately. I, at once, ceased to take the mickey out of the navy and fervently wished them early success against the Chinese gun, though I still retained a sneaking admiration for the artillery piece.

The Yanks tried, oh how they tried; the little gun became almost an obsession with them. The secret of the Chinese crew was their inconsistency. Some days they would not appear at all, on other days they made three or four forays against the assembled US ships. Part of my delight at the episode, of course, that I was out of range of the gun. It was not handled very accurately; in fact it rarely hit anything, but I admired their perseverance and bottle!

'Dave, quick, come and have a look.'

I clambered out of my little hole and headed towards the hilltop toilet. As I arrived, breathless with anticipation, I gazed across the harbour. 'Christ, they are taking this a little seriously,' I shouted at the group of assembled Commandos. There, majestic in its enormity, was a huge, and I do mean huge, American battleship. It was the USS Missouri, 45,000 tons of irritable Yankee steel. It was armed with nine 16-inch guns, the biggest naval guns in the world, capable of throwing a one-ton shell from each barrel. It slowly eased its way across the harbour until it was broadside to the hills containing the cheeky Chinese bastards. High above the valuable ship droned dozens of American aircraft, guarding their personification of naval might. The huge turrets traversed until they were pointing threateningly at the hills ashore, very close range for such sophisticated armament. I prayed for their success; better for them to do it rather than we Marines. I did not fancy, for one moment, climbing up the hills liberally dotted with unfriendly Chinamen, to destroy their bloody gun, even if I found it!

With an ear-shattering roar, nine tons of high explosive winged across the short distance to explode with devastating power on the hill. Within the next few minutes six broadsides were fired by the *Missouri*. The area that had hidden the Chinese gun was wreathed in heavy smoke, which, as it cleared, revealed the hill to be completely battered over its entire area. The destroyers whooped their sirens in triumph. The guns of the battleship regained their fore and aft stance as, almost modestly, the battleship slowly cruised out of the harbour. There was smug satisfaction written over the entire incident. The Stars and Stripes had fluttered bravely in the gentle summer breeze. Had I been American, thrills of pride would have rippled up and down my spine. As the bows of the great ship pointed to the entrance to the harbour, we, on the hill top, pleased at the Yank's determination and relieved of the need for any further action, cheered madly.

The cheers, however, faded into disbelief as, 'Pop!'

A little spurt of water cascaded just abaft the stern of the *Missouri*. It couldn't be! It was! The bloody Chinese gun had fired a passing shot from the decimated hills. As usual, they missed, but their morale must have been lifted beyond measure as the *Missouri*, with apparent chagrin, raised steam and sped disconsolately out to sea. Our cheers faded to a groan. The Yankee aircraft, which were guarding the *Missouri* from above, swooped angrily down on the hill and gave it the entire business . . . rockets, bombs and napalm. We knew they were wasting their time, it would all be to no avail. The little cave appeared to be proof against all sorts of dive-bombing attacks. We stood about in disbelief, conversation stilled.

In the distance we heard the muted roar of aircraft engines. They sounded somehow different, so much so that for a brief moment I thought that Chinese planes may have slipped through the superior air barrier, put up by the Yanks at the border, not too far south at the Yalu River. Our eyes followed the directions of our ears and we gazed to seaward. There, at sea level, going like the clappers out of hell, were nine aircraft. Realisation suddenly dawned and we cheered with the enthusiasm of a cup final crowd, berets flew into the air, for there were the target roundels of red, white and blue. They were Seafires of the Royal Navy Fleet Air Arm. Brother British. They sped across the harbour, hedgehopping the islands, heading straight for the hills containing the bloody gun. They were obviously hoping that a low-level attack would enable their rockets to enter the cave; everything else had been tried. Tracer fire zoomed up to meet them as they approached. As they eased up and gained height, rocket trails continued on the course they had previously maintained. With a series of large rumbling explosions the rockets exploded against the hill and the British aircraft turned back and passed over us as they headed back to their aircraft carrier, HMS *Unicorn*. We waved and jumped about as the pilots raised their arms in salute. Then as quickly as they had arrived, they had gone. I almost burst forth into *Rule Britannia,* but I desisted, because I was sure, that had I done so, an American MP would have appeared from nowhere and smote me mightily on the head with his truncheon!

From that day on we never heard from the little gun again. The Yanks, of course, claimed the *Missouri* and the US Air Force had done the trick. Our response was, 'Bollocks . . . it was our lads, the Royal Navy pilots who finished the bastard off!'

I missed the little gun. It had not been accurate, had done little damage, but its sauciness had appealed to me. I have a sneaking suspicion that it quietly shoved off, without damage, knowing that the ensuing arguments would cause many a rift between the British and American antagonists, it was a bloody nuisance right up to the end!

A pleasant sequel to the incident was that, some weeks later, we received a message from HMS *Unicorn*, inviting some of the commandos for a break, to spend a few days on the ship for a rest and clean up. I broke the habit of a lifetime and volunteered. Some 20 of us were transported far out to sea in an American destroyer and then transferred to the carrier. The welcome we received was out of this world. The lower deck treated us like kings. We relished in the delights of about six showers a day. I presume the crew were quite pleased about this, as I feel sure we smelled a little high after months on the island. We were fed until our gluttony was satiated and joy were issued with a daily ration of Navy rum; lovely. It is an old naval custom that, for special occasions, members of the crew will donate 'sippers' from their rum ration for deserving causes. I had many sippers for the few days we were on board and spent some winsome hours recovering. It was infinitely preferable to Gilhoully's concoction and I had no fear that someone would whisper in my ear, 'You won't go blind . . . I think!'

I enjoyed the hairiness of the landings and takeoffs which we watched from the deck of the carrier. However even this evoked sad memories. My school pal Keith had joined the Fleet Air Arm at the same time that I signed on with the marines. He became a pilot and died when his aircraft overshot the flight deck during the war. The visit reinforced one of my pet hates, Royal Navy officers. I found their arrogance towards the lower deck offensive. The discipline in the Royal Marines was much severer in some respects but administered in a very different way and our governors shared our hardships and engendered a certain respect from the troops. Had I had a Royal Navy officer in charge through the Korean campaign, I feel sure he would have returned to UK wounded, with an undignified small-arms wound somewhere about the fleshy portions in the rear!

All things end and we had, after a few days, to leave the Unicorn and return to our islands, to be met with the distressing news that one of our landing craft had broken down and drifted onto the mainland with a troop sergeant major and three marines aboard. They were taken prisoner.

The island of Taedo was a leper colony and considered with some awe by the commandos as a definite 'no go' area. In any case the island had been left severely isolated, both by the Chinese and by ourselves. However, we British being considered to be gentlemen and not at all sneaky had, some months earlier, quietlyevacuated the lepers to an island further south, brain-washed our troops into the knowledge that leprosy was not infectious, and with a sneakiness of which even Billy Bunter would have been proud, took advantage of the Chinese belief that we would play the game and landed a troop of commandos. The nearest I had been to the place was when I had tussled with the Russian sea mine and then from an adjoining island I had felt uneasy picturing little leprococci germs leaping and cavorting across at me!

You may think that we had been a little naughty sneaking the lepers away, but it gave us the opportunity to surprise the enemy and give them a bloody nose with fire from the island. There is an old saying which applies to this situation. 'Do it to them before the bastards can do it to you!' On this occasion we did just that.

The occupation of the leper colony meant that, at last, all of the islands were occupied by us, the beaches were mined, shelters dug and we were engaging the Chinese with both gunfire and constant landings from aggressive marines. We were accomplishing that for which we had planned,. because the Korean spies who flitted between the islands and the mainland gave us the information that large numbers of Chinese formations were being moved to the Wonsan area, which meant fewer men at the front on the 38th parallel. As the mainland became more fortified it was increasingly difficult to raid. It must be realised that the types of landings and the vessels we were using made opposed landings well-nigh impossible and we were constantly searching for unguarded areas to harass.

Once a week our supplies were ferried out to us from a Yankee destroyer by landing craft. We were, without doubt, cadgers *extraordinaire* and adopted many ruses to fiddle extra out of the Yanks. On Yodo we kept a log of the numbers painted on the sides of the American destroyers. When a strange vessel appeared we homed in on it like vultures and bled them dry, with all the other Yankee ships watching amused and silent. They had all been conned in turn and would have been disappointed if one of their ships had been spared. So we lived reasonably well on official and purloined supplies. The Yanks did, however, on one occasion have the last laugh.

A new destroyer entered the bay; at once we gathered the cadging team together, consisting of the gauntest men of the unit to reinforce our story that we were starving. One or two blood-stained bandages and they were off. Success, as always, greeted their startling appearance and laden to the gunwales with goodies the jubilant cadgers headed for the shore. It was imperative that the stores should be landed and stowed unseen by the officers, who would have placed an embargo on our cadging activities. They may well have been turning a blind eye to our initiative in obtaining luxuries but, in case not, various lookouts were in position. It was fairly obvious that this particular expedition had been especially successful for the jubilant crew were punching the sky with delight as the craft drew close to the beach. With about 300 yards to go the Chinese artillery ashore decided to have a little pop at the Yank navy. Their shells dropped amongst the destroyers who proceeded to perform their customary 'war dance'. Our landing craft increased speed to get ashore a little quicker.

From a spot ashore, it was never discovered where exactly, a voice boomed forth, 'Down ramp!' It was alleged afterwards that the voice sounded suspiciously like mine. I denied this emphatically for many weeks after. The marine in charge of the ramp mechanism reacted automatically to the shouted order and wound down the ramp with customary speed. As he did so the forward motion of the craft scooped in the sea and, with some alacrity, the craft started to sink by the bows.

The troops ashore watched aghast as their ill-gotten gains headed for the bottom of the sea. The stern of the boat pointed to the sky. The cadgers were all swimming towards the shore with the exception of the coxswain who was clinging to the after deck. As the craft started its imitation of the titanic, the same loud voice was heard to shout, 'Salute you bastard . . . salute !'

The figure clinging to the stern, looked towards the shore, scrambled uncertainly to his feet on the slopping deck, remained at attention and saluted as the craft slid between the waves. The final scenario was just his head and hand still at the salute poking above the surface as the boat settled on the bottom. His discipline was magnificent, it was, 'the boy stood on the burning deck' all over again. We managed to recover some of our ill-gotten gains but the vast majority of the stores floated away, never to be seen again. The one indication of the delight of the destroyer crews, as our final cadging operation came to its ignominious end, were hearty cheers echoing across the bay as the craft sank, none more heartily than those from the new destroyer which had been so recently conned. We never tried it again!

CHAPTER TWENTY-TWO

Good Riddance

Raiding in the vicinity of Wonsan became increasingly difficult. We decided once again to try further afield and on 27th September a group of us embarked on the USS *Wantuck*, an assault personnel destroyer. Our intention was to travel north and attack the railway line near the coast at Sonjin, using the rubber-boat technique and, of course operating at night. Whilst we were thus engaged in a smaller group, in canoes, we were to land to the north of our position and try some mischief on any reinforcements heading in our direction. Alas, times had changed. After swanning about paddling for hours in an attempt to find an unguarded beach it was discovered that the entire coastline was heavily defended and we could not get ashore. We were the victims of our own past successes. Every Chinaman watching the coast was one less at the front. Considering that there were less than 200 of us, it did seem that we were tying down a fair number of Chinese troops. The canoes, even further north, had managed to slip ashore and lay some mines on a road near the coast. They beetled off at the sound of approaching trucks and were pleased, as they paddled furiously away under fire, to hear explosions indicating that they at least had had some success on that dark night.

Early in October we received what was to us, sad news: Duggie was returning to the United Kingdom. He was a man tremendously admired by the blokes at the bottom and sharp end of the scale. Admiration is not easily given or attained with troops of the calibre of 41 Commando; he had, however, captured their complete loyalty and we were sad to hear that he was on his way. He was eventually to go to the US Marine Corps depot at Quantico in the States to give them the benefit of his experience with us.

Winter was slowly approaching and a gentle chill reminded us of the ferocity of the winter before, I was not looking forward at all to spending another freezing time in North Korea. The Commando by now had received a number of reinforcements from 3 Commando Brigade, which was winning a war in Malaya against foes of the same political persuasion as our Korean and Chinese antagonists.

The war in Korea was now a complete stalemate. Armies dug in opposite one another on the 38th parallel, which was the original border between North and South Korea. We were probably the only United Nations land forces north of the parallel. Our chances of staying in such inhospitable surroundings throughout the deep winter seemed quite slim.

There were no women on the island and life had been fairly monastic. It therefore became a topic for considerable conjecture when one of the commandos, after a visit to Petty Officer Gilhoully, was discovered to be the proud possessor of a fairly minor version of venereal disease. Like the Virgin Mary he claimed that his condition was in no way attributable to sexual intercourse. But unlike the response to the Virgin Mary's story, no one believed him. Virgin birth may have been plausible to believers, but under no circumstances was Virgin Venereal Disease even considered a likely prospect. He was greeted after a journey on the casualty boat, with even more jubilation than I had had with my napalm ring and had even met the nauseating unofficial spokesman, who had regaled the story to all and sundry on the Yankee destroyer. The mystery was never solved. There were not any sheep on the island and he did not posses a pair of wellington boots, so his enigmatic smile hid a story which would have been worth a fortune in the *Sun* newspaper . The only possible solution was that he had met an accommodating female during one of the raids. This seemed unlikely under the circumstances but he never said! He was denied the use of the toilet on the hilltop and had to dig his own little pit. Still, it is well known that venereal disease can only be transmitted by toilet seats to two classes of person: chaplains and officers. Everyone else has it away to contact the ailment. Such is life.

Our new boss man was Colonel Grant. I was never to be involved in an operation under his command, for, as November chilled its way across Korea I received the first piece of 'good news' that 'Bad News Percy' had ever imparted. We were leaving the islands and going back to Japan. Not the unit – they were to stay – but the members of the original unit that had flown from London Airport so long ago. The remainder were to stay and slog out the winter. Good luck to them! They would need it. My one anxiety was that they were gathering together, in Japan, the most experienced members of the unit. Had they got plans for us? Oh Christ, I hoped not!

As the bobbing landing craft drew away from the beach the following day, with other fellows who had served together from the very beginning, I looked back at the island which had been my home for so long. The scenario was exactly as it had been on our arrival, with the exception that it had been summer when we had landed and today was a crisp winter's morning. The islands looked lonely and vulnerable against the bulk of the mainland, I wondered how we had survived so long under such circumstances. I knew how Robinson Crusoe must have felt as he left his island home: delight tinged with regret, very slight regret, at the passing of a way of life to which he had become accustomed. I gazed at Yodo. There, perched on the highest crest, was the wooden box which had served as a grandstand toilet. How many relaxed hours I had spent there watching the war go by. I waved a casual goodbye to the American destroyers, still keeping watch with the occasional excitement of a 'war dance'. I remembered the bulk of the magnificent *Missouri* as it shamefacedly skulked out of the bay with the splash of the little Chinese gun up its arse. Ah . . . the little Chinese gun . . . if the enemy could be recalled with something akin to affection that little gun could. I almost hoped that the crew survived, they deserved to!

As we clambered up the scrambling nets and aboard the American transport I felt the tremendous luxury, denied me for many months, of complete relaxation from tension. Once on deck I turned my eyes to the dark sombre mainland of Korea, by now a distant shadow on the horizon. What a God-awful country it was. I could think of nothing whatsoever in its favour. The terrain was hilly and inhospitable, the weather was ghastly and its women, without doubt the ugliest females in the world! We had all fought and suffered for it. Many good friends lay beneath its cold ground and many were still there as prisoners of war. For every one of us that survived, one of our unit was either dead, wounded or a prisoner of war. The mainland slowly disappeared in the haze, whether caused by increasing the distance or eye moisture was hard to stay. The evening before we left Yodo I had visited the quiet glade where Binnie and Lieutenant Harwood were buried. I had bid them farewell and thanked Binnie for the many happy moments his sense of humour engendered.

Goodbye Korea . . . I hope!

We returned to Sasebo in Japan, the current base camp of the Commando. I was still a little puzzled and suspicious as to what exactly the powers that be had in mind for us. However, there were certain priorities to be taken care of, therefore, Bill, Gerry and I savoured the somewhat shabby delights of the area. Not in any way to be compared with the ecstasies of Tokyo but at least a considerable improvement over the conditions we had endured for months on the islands. Our condition quickly deteriorated with the excesses of the flesh and our financial position rapidly became worse. Gerry, who had managed, God knows how, to obtain another parka, constantly reminded us that he only possessed one parka and watched it like a hawk!

'Gather round chaps.' I visibly paled as Percy appeared. I searched his expression for a sign of comfort; I wanted reassurance that he was not, yet again, going to lead us on some warlike endeavour. I was pissed off with war, I had had enough for a while. I searched in vain; he looked stern and business-like. It looked as though 'Bad News Percy' was going to strike again. I should have known, all the most experienced marines were here, no greenhorns or replacements. Sod it, it looked bad.

Percy cleared his throat, perused the piece of paper in his hand, looked at each one of us in turn, and said, 'We are going home!'

My heart jumped. I had made it, I had survived and was going home. I was surrounded by beaming smiles, there were no cheers, just absolute delight glowing from us all. Percy was smiling, he had squeezed every inch of suspense out of the situation but now we knew!

It was time for our last 'run ashore' in Japan. I had tucked away sufficient cash to purchase a present for my mother and sister Maureen, I had determined to buy them each a local speciality which was a tea service of superb china, wafer thin, made locally by craftsmen and packed and despatched with consummate skill. Though not exactly expensive by European standards, the money I wished to use for the purchase could have provided a full intoxicating measure of booze. Bill argued with me for hours to release the funds for our mutual benefit. His argument had some merit, as I had assisted him to spend his 'present' money on alcohol a few short days earlier. I ignored his frantic supplications which continued up to the moment that I stood in the Sasebo store clutching the money in my sweaty hands. I ordered and paid for the china, which arrived safely and unbroken in the UK some weeks later. Though it curbed the amount of celebratory booze we could consume I was pleased that I had been able to display a fair amount of family filiality.

'You rotten bastard, you helped me spend mine,' Bill moaned and complained unendingly.

However, as always, I ended the loser, for, about a year later, in Liverpool, as Bill and my sister posed for their wedding photographs, he winked at me and whispered, 'With all her worldly goods she has me endowed ... thanks for the Sasebo tea service!'

'You rotten bastard,' I whispered back, defeated yet again.

At last, my dreams had come true, I positively galloped up the gangway and aboard the ship before some officious bastard changed their mind. I disappeared into the between deck labyrinth of RMS *Georgic*, a very large and sumptuously appointed liner. Having journeyed miserably, on troopships before I was pleasantly surprised. The vessel had been specially chartered to carry emigrants from the UK to Australia on the outward journey, and troops home from Korea before returning to its normal passenger duties. The cabins, which were four-berthers, were roomy and comfortable. From the cabin next door a voice rang out, 'Dave, I've just heard. They have stewardesses aboard to look after us.'

'You're joking?'

'I'm not, it's true'

As he spoke a fairly presentable female, attractive in a form of ship's uniform, meandered past, stopped at the cabin next door and said, 'I am your stewardess for the journey. If there is anything you need you just have to ring.' She fluttered her eyelashes, turned and walked away down the passage with what I thought was a slightly provocative twitch. The four occupants, jaws agape, slowly regained their senses. She had been the first British female they had seen for many moons. I could almost see their imaginations running riot. They were indeed happy.

'Wonder what yours will be like!' With a long six week journey ahead, so did I!

The four of us waited in the cabin, agog. We heard the tip-tap of delicately shod feet which slowed and stopped outside our cabin door. There was a gentle knock and I opened the door expectantly.

He stood there, hand on hip. 'I am your steward for the journey, if there is anything you might need, you only have to ring!' He turned and minced off. Of the six stewards responsible for our deck, five were crumpet and we were the only cabin to be serviced by a handsome young man!!

We made frantic attempts to change cabins, to no avail. In the event, it made little difference to us. Most of the women onboard, including the stewardesses, had better fish to fry than the peasants on the troop decks, however temporary the liaison may have been. As for our personal steward, he was a magnificently efficient chap, who, in response to our anxious protestations as to our heterosexuality, said, 'Don't worry, dear. I wouldn't touch you lot with a barge pole. Not only are you uncouth, you are all so fucking ugly!'

I was not really settled until we had passed Singapore and were well on our way through the Indian Ocean. The reason, of course, was that 3 Commando Brigade was stationed in Malaysia and fighting a war against communist insurgents. It would only take a radio message and we would have been ashore involved, yet again, in circumstances where people would keep shooting things at us. Perhaps the Admiralty had forgotten about us?

At long last we arrived at the Suez Canal, the domain of the Egyptian officer who had started the whole sorry story. As the huge liner passed slowly between the close banks of the canal many of us, including a number of the army nurses, were leaning lazily against the rail enjoying the proximity of the desert sands and the warm sun.

It was then I saw my first Egyptian standing on the bank. A swarthy, unwashed man, middle aged, wearing a long garment reaching to his ankles. He looked fairly evil and glared at the symbol of British Imperialism as it floated slowly through his fair land. As he saw the nurses leaning over the rail he started to trot to keep pace with them. Our speed was, however, somewhat deceptive because he began to lose ground. He stamped his bare feet angrily. One of the nurses, in a high-pitched, posh accent, called out, 'Shuftie kush!'

With that the Egyptian bent over, gripped the hem of his scruffy garment and as he raised his arms to allah, he also raised his robe revealing to all and sundry that though Egyptians may not be over-endowed with common sense or courage, Allah had obviously compensated them by an issue of wedding tackle any Christian would have been proud of.

'Hooray . . . he's shuftie kushed,' shrieked the nurse. She was offensively loud and thoroughly enjoying herself. However, she had furthered my education a little. I was now absolutely positive that the Egyptian Officer at Sandown had not called 'shuftie kush': it would have been most inappropriate at the time!

With us on board, were a number of soldiers who had served with the Commonwealth Division in Korea. From them we had learned that they had had a very hard time during the Chinese offensive. It is strange that when you are actively involved in a small section of a war, you haven't a clue what is going on elsewhere. Having spoken to some of the men from the Gloucester's and the Eighth Hussars for a very short while we agreed we would not bore one another with our respective stories. We were all going home, that was all that mattered. Later I read avidly a great deal of literature about the British Army in Korea: they really did have a tough time.

One morning as I meandered to the upper deck it was quite chilly and it was raining. 'Ah,' I thought, 'we are nearly home.' The January chill bore little resemblance to the extreme North Korean cold, but there was a moisture to the chill which was fairly miserable.

At last the day arrived. Eagerly I searched the horizon . . . there it was . . . England. Even its silhouette was gentler than its Korean counterpart. I was so desperately pleased to see it. We were crowded against the ship's rail but each of us was alone, our emotions and thoughts private. Once again I revelled in the fact that I was so lucky to be coming home. The 97 men out of the original 200 who were either dead, wounded, prisoner of war or missing, crowded my mind. It was devastating to think of it.

We were entering the River Mersey and I could pick out the familiar sights of the city, in which I had spent my childhood. It was dingy, the stone of the buildings smoke-stained and ugly . . . it was beautiful! As the ship slowly drew alongside the quay there was no Falklands welcome. Just a few dockers and one or two military representatives of the units on board. We could have been returning from a cross-channel day trip. Within minutes of strolling down the gangplank I had been processed by customs, had all sorts of forms stamped and checked and clutching my leave pass, was standing in a bus queue waiting to be transported to the outskirts of Liverpool where my family lived.

As we of the Commando had parted, some to the railway

station and others to buses, a few clasped handshakes and muttered, 'See you mate.'

The Unit was no more.

I had one final task to perform. After some weeks of leave I headed for London, ostensibly to meet Bill Taylor and his family. Whilst visiting I remembered that one of the young lads of the assault engineers had lived nearby. He had at first been reported as missing, but nothing had been heard of him since. I wanted badly to see his parents and perhaps be of some comfort to them. They were not on the telephone so it was just a case of knocking on the door unannounced and unexpected.

I walked along the clean street of a large council estate consisting of neat semi-detached houses with immaculate gardens. I thought of the lad, these were streets in which, as a kid, he had kicked a football about. What on earth had the security of South Korea to do with these quiet west London estates?

As I walked up the garden path at the address I saw the briefest of movement of a lace curtain. I was not in uniform. I knocked on the door. It was opened by a sad-faced middle-aged lady and, looking over her shoulder was the pert face of a girl, obviously Bill's younger sister.

'Yes, can I help you?' Her voice had a slight touch of cockney without the harshness associated with the accent.

'I am a friend of your son's. I've been home some weeks and I wondered if you would mind me coming to see you.'

She stepped back a little,

'I have no news for you I am afraid,' I hastily added.

'Please come in.' She stepped aside and I followed the young girl along a narrow passage into a room which was furnished in exactly the same way as my parents home in Liverpool. Nothing posh, but all paid for.

There, on the mantelpiece, in the place of honour at the

centre stood a framed photograph of a young man, Green beret carefully positioned with the badge properly just above his left eye. His shoulder slightly turned to reveal the unit insignia, 'Royal Marines' with the word 'Commando' looped underneath it. He looked so young. I felt a lump in my throat and was conscious of the aura of sadness about the home. I felt guilty for having survived.

She was kind and inquisitive and asked questions of me as to how her son had been. I reassured her that up until that battle of Kotori he had been very well and that I had not seen him during the actual battle. She seemed pleased and comforted as our conversation unfolded. As the talk continued to the chink of tea cups I made the agonising discovery that she had two sons and had lost the elder one in the second world war.

Suddenly, out of the blue, she said, 'Mind you, the reporter from the *Daily Worker* was ever so kind and helpful.' Her eyes brighter suddenly.

'The *Daily Worker*?' I was surprised. The story that unfolded was so sad.

Some weeks after receiving the telegram informing her of her son being reported missing in Korea, she had been visited by a man who stated that he was a reporter from the *Daily Worker* a communist paper since renamed *The Morning Star*. This man had informed her that his newspaper had correspondents on duty on the North Korean side reporting from the communist angle. He stated that he could probably obtain information about her son through the newspapers correspondent. This she grabbed at as a way to ease her terrible stress and she agreed. Some days later the man returned and asked her to write a short letter, condemning the fact that her son had been used in the fight in Korea, which she did. At this stage she thought that it would help her receive information regarding her son if she, unsolicited, joined the Communist Party. This she did and was welcomed into the fold. Eventually, through official British sources she was informed that he was a prisoner of war in Korea. From that moment she neither saw nor heard from the *Daily Worker* and had no further contact with the Communist Party. I was horrified at this story and told her so. She begged me not to make any fuss as she felt it might jeopardize the future of her son. I kept very quiet about it and have done so for 30 years.

When the prisoners of war were finally released some years later, her son was not among them and is presumed dead. I had had my doubts as to the usefulness of the Korean episode from a personal point of view. Those doubts were removed when I heard the sad tale of the commando's mother! I am glad that I was able without much impact, to have a pop at a system capable of such activity.

Roll of Honour

41st Independent Commando, Royal Marines. The following list of those who were killed in action, died of wounds or, in captivity, died as a result of the treatment they received.

Captain R. N. Parkinson Cumine RM
Surgeon L.T. Knock RN
Lieut. J. G. Harwood RM
A/PO J. A. Tate RM
Sgt. C. E. Barnes RM
Sgt. R. G. Davies RM
Corpl. P. B. Babb RM
Corpl. J. E. Belsey RM
Corpl. C. R. Hill RM
Corpl. R. Southworth RM
Corpl. C. E. Trot RM
L/SBA. D. Raines RN
Marine G. Aherne
Marine A. J. Aldrich
Marine E. Garner
Marine J. L. Graham
Marine L. A. Heard
Marine S. E. Hills
Marine K. D. Hitchman
Marine W. L. Jauncy
Marine P. R. Jones
Marine J. McCourt
Marine H. Melling
Marine J. Needs
Marine R. Nichols
Marine S. Skelton
Marine E. Strain
Marine D. W. Stray
Marine W. A. Walker
Marine R. Wooldridge
Marine K. Wyeth

In addition to those who died a further 26 were taken prisoner of war during the battle between Hagaru and Kotori, of which nine are on the list of dead. During the entire campaign a further 43 members of the unit were wounded.

The casualty ratio over the campaign for the men of 41 Independent Commando was almost exactly 50 per cent. A high price by any standard. It is to these magnificent men that I dedicate this book.

List of Illustrations

		Page no.
1.	USS Perch	193
2.	The Author, Brady, Kowloon, Hong Kong.	193
3.	British Ambassador inspecting a rubber assault boat.	194
4.	Commandos joining an assault for a night raid.	194
5.	Boarding an assault ship, Yokasuka Harbour.	195
6a–d.	Amtraks at Hungnam, North Korea.	196
7.	Author at Kure, Japan, before the battle of the Chosin Reservoir.	198
8.	Col. Drysdale's Jeep, Hell Fire Valley, where he was wounded.	199
9a.	Commandos breakthrough at Hagaru to link up with USMC.	199
9b.	After the battle, Masan.	200
10.	41 Ind. Com. Briefing for Sonjin daylight raid.	201
11a–b.	Assault ship discharges Amtraks for the Sonjin raid.	202
12a.	Landing on the beach, Sonjin.	203
12b.	The daylight assault.	204
12c.	Waiting to attack.	204
13a.	Sonjin Village.	205
13b.	Evacuating the villagers of Sonjin.	205
14.	Awaiting re-deployment, Sonjin.	206
15.	8-inch shells fired by the cruiser, USS Saint Paul in support of the Sonjin landing.	206

	Page no.
16a–b. Planting primary 'Beehive' charges.	207
17a–d. Placing the main charges to destroy the railway embankment.	208
18a–b. After the 'bang' and prior to anti-personel mines to deter repair.	210
19. Preparing to re-embark after the Sonjin raid.	211
20. Practicing beach landings with Amtraks.	211

> The Sonjin raid was carried out by the entire Commando Unit, with air and sea power support, and executed in daylight. All other assaults by 41 Independent Commando were carried out by unsupported, small raiding parties at night.

THE SONJIN RAID

1. USS Perch

2. The Author, Brady, Kowloon, Hong Kong.

3. British Ambassador inspecting a rubber assault boat.

4. Commandos joining an assault for a night raid.

5. Boarding an assault ship, Yokasuka Harbour.

a.

b.

THE SONJIN RAID 197

c.

d.

6. Amtraks at Hungnam, North Korea.

7. Author at Kure, Japan, before the battle of the Chosin Reservoir.

8. Col. Drysdale's Jeep, Hell Fire Valley, where he was wounded.

9a. Commandos breakthrough at Hagaru to link up with USMC.

9b. After the battle, Masan.

10. 41 Ind. Com. Briefing for Sonjin daylight raid.

11a. Assault ship discharges Amtraks for the Sonjin raid.

THE SONJIN RAID

11b. Assault ship discharges Amtraks for the Sonjin raid.

12a. Landing on the beach, Sonjin.

12b. The daylight assault.

12c. Waiting to attack.

13a. Sonjin Village.

13b. Evacuating the villagers of Sonjin.

14. Awaiting re-deployment, Sonjin.

15. 8-inch shells fired by the cruiser, USS Saint Paul in support of the Sonjin landing.

a.

b.

16. Planting primary 'Beehive' charges.

a.

b.

c.

d.

17. Placing the main charges to destroy the railway embankment.

a.

b.

18. After the 'bang' and prior to anti-personel mines to deter repair.

THE SONJIN RAID 211

19. Preparing to re-embark after the Sonjin raid.

20. Practicing beach landings with Amtraks.